HOW TO TALK TO ANYONE WITH CONFIDENCE

Unlocking the Secret to
Overcoming Social Anxiety

Michelle Mann

TABLE OF CONTENTS

Chapter 8

INTRODUCTION

DEFINING CHARISMA AND ITS IMPORTANCE IN TODAY'S SOCIETY

In today's interconnected and socially-driven world, effective communication and the ability to connect with others have become essential skills. Whether it's forming new friendships, building professional networks, or navigating social gatherings, the art of talking to anyone with ease has the potential to profoundly impact our personal and professional lives. However, for many individuals, the presence of social anxiety poses a significant obstacle, hindering their ability to engage in conversations and establish meaningful connections.

Social anxiety is a common phenomenon characterized by feelings of apprehension, self-consciousness, and fear of judgment in social situations. It can manifest as sweaty palms, a racing heart, or an overwhelming urge to avoid social interactions altogether. The fear of saying the wrong thing, being judged, or simply not knowing how to initiate or sustain conversations can create a barrier to building relationships and seizing opportunities.

But what if there were secrets to overcoming this social anxiety? What if there were tools and techniques that could empower individuals to break free from the constraints of their fears and unleash the power of effective communication? This is where the concept of charisma enters the picture. Charisma, often considered a natural gift possessed by a select few, is not an innate quality exclusive to a fortunate minority. It is an art that can be learned, honed, and mastered. Charisma is the ability to engage, influence, and inspire others through effective communication and interpersonal skills. It goes beyond mere charm or magnetism; it encompasses the ability to connect deeply with individuals, leaving a lasting impact on their lives.

In this book, "How to Talk to Anyone: The Secret to Overcoming Social Anxiety," we embark on a journey to unlock the power of effective communication through the art of charisma. We will explore the intricacies of social anxiety, dissect the components that make up charisma, and provide practical strategies and actionable advice to help individuals develop their own charismatic abilities. Throughout the following chapters, we will delve into the psychology and science behind charisma, examining its neurological and evolutionary foundations. We will discover the benefits of possessing charisma, not only in terms of personal relationships but also in enhancing our overall health and well-being. It is important to acknowledge that charisma, like any other tool, can also be misused. We will shed light on the potential dark side of charisma, exploring how it can be used for manipulation and control.

Equipped with this understanding, we will guide you through the journey of cultivating charisma within yourself. We will provide you with practical tips, techniques, and exercises to develop the key traits and behaviors that charismatic individuals possess. You will learn how to project confidence, charm, and authenticity, creating genuine connections and captivating audiences. Furthermore, we will explore how to leverage your newfound charisma to be more persuasive, influential, and successful in various aspects of life. Whether it's mastering the art of storytelling, understanding the power of body language, or employing effective persuasion techniques, you will gain the tools to navigate social interactions with confidence and impact. Additionally, we will address the importance of building solid relationships based on charm, empathy, and trust. We will delve into the foundations of confidence, offering guidance on overcoming self-doubt and managing social anxiety. Along the way, we will provide you with valuable resources, recommended readings, and answers to frequently asked questions to support your continued growth and development in the realm of charisma.

By the end of this book, you will have gained a comprehensive understanding of charisma, its applications, and its potential to transform your social interactions. You will be equipped with practical skills and strategies to overcome social anxiety, connect with others authentically, and navigate social situations with ease. Now, let us embark on this journey together, as we uncover the secrets to mastering the art of charisma and unleash your true potential in conversations and connections.

CHAPTER 1

THE PSYCHOLOGY OF CHARISMA: HOW BEING CHARISMATIC CAN MAKEYOU MORE SUCCESSFUL IN LIFE

Charisma is a captivating quality that goes beyond surface-level charm. It is a multifaceted phenomenon rooted in the intricate workings of human psychology. In this chapter, we delve deep into the psychological underpinnings of charisma, exploring how it can enhance your personal and professional life. By understanding the psychological foundations of charisma, you will gain valuable insights into human interactions and discover how to harness the power of charisma to achieve remarkable success. At its essence, charisma is not an inherent trait possessed exclusively by a select few individuals. It is a skill set that can be learned, honed, and mastered. By examining the psychology of charisma, we can unravel the traits and behaviors commonly associated with charismatic individuals and explore how you can cultivate these attributes within yourself.

Emotional intelligence lies at the core of charisma. Charismatic individuals possess a heightened sense of empathy and an exceptional ability to understand and manage both their own emotions and the emotions of others. They have a keen intuition for nonverbal cues and are skilled at active listening, making others feel heard and understood. By developing your emotional intelligence, you can deepen your connections with others, forge genuine relationships, and create a positive impact on those around you. Self-confidence is another crucial aspect of charisma. Charismatic individuals exude self-assurance, which naturally attracts others to them. They possess a firm belief in their abilities and maintain a positive self-image. Building self-confidence requires self-reflection, self-acceptance, and the cultivation of a growth mindset. By recognizing your strengths, embracing your uniqueness, and working on areas of improvement, you can boost your self-confidence and project an aura of authenticity and competence.

Effective communication is a fundamental component of charisma. Charismatic individuals possess exceptional verbal and nonverbal communication skills. They articulate their thoughts with clarity and conviction, utilizing compelling storytelling techniques, captivating body language, and persuasive language. By honing your communication skills, you can express your ideas effectively, engage your audience, and leave a lasting impact. Charismatic individuals also demonstrate a remarkable ability to adapt to various social situations and connect with people from all walks of life. They possess a genuine interest in others, demonstrate empathy, and create a sense of belonging. By developing your social skills, embracing diversity, and cultivating an open mind, you can expand your social circles, build robust networks, and create opportunities for personal and professional growth.

The psychology of charisma encompasses the understanding of human behavior, motivation, and the dynamics of interpersonal relationships. By delving into the intricacies of charisma, you gain profound insights into the power dynamics at play in social interactions. You become aware of the influence of body language, facial expressions, and tone of voice. This heightened awareness allows you to navigate social situations with finesse and authenticity, establishing connections that are both meaningful and impactful. Furthermore, charisma holds the potential to unlock doors of opportunity. It can make you more successful in various aspects of life, ranging from personal relationships to professional endeavors. Charismatic individuals possess the ability to inspire and influence others. They have a natural magnetism that attracts people to their cause, enabling them to form alliances, build teams, and achieve shared goals. By harnessing the power of charisma, you can become a persuasive leader, a trusted collaborator, and an influential figure in your chosen field.

In the subsequent chapters of this book, we will explore each component of charisma in greater detail, providing practical strategies, tips, and exercises to help you develop and embody charisma in your everyday interactions. We will guide you on a transformative journey, unraveling the secrets of emotional intelligence, self-confidence, effective communication, and social adaptability. By embracing the psychology of charisma, you will unlock a world of possibilities . Your personal relationships will deepen, your professional network will expand, and your overall success will soar to new heights. Whether you aspire to excel in public speaking, leadership roles, or social gatherings, charisma will serve as your guiding light.

As we navigate through the intricacies of charisma, we invite you to reflect on your own journey. What qualities do you admire in charismatic individuals? How can you cultivate those traits within yourself? Through introspection, practice, and an unwavering commitment to personal growth, you have the power to unleash your charismatic potential and create a lasting impact on the world around you. Join us on this transformative journey as we unravel the secrets of the psychology of charisma and explore how being charismatic can make you more successful in life.

CHAPTER 2

THE SCIENCE OF CHARISMA: THE NEUROLOGICAL AND EVOLUTIONARY BASIS FOR CHARISMA

Charisma, as we have come to know it, is not simply a mysterious quality that some individuals possess. It has a scientific basis rooted in our neurological and evolutionary makeup. In this chapter, we embark on a captivating exploration of the science behind charisma, unveiling the intricate mechanisms that underlie this remarkable human trait. By delving into the neurological and evolutionary aspects of human communication, we will provide you with a deeper understanding of why charisma holds such sway in our interactions, and how you can leverage this knowledge to enhance your own charismatic presence.

At the core of the science of charisma lies the study of the brain. Neurologists and cognitive scientists have delved into the neural pathways and brain regions that contribute to charismatic behavior. Through advanced imaging techniques such as functional magnetic resonance imaging (fMRI), researchers have gained insights into the brain activity associated with charisma. These studies reveal that charismatic individuals exhibit heightened activity in regions associated with social cognition, emotional processing, and reward systems. One key area of the brain that plays a pivotal role in charisma is the prefrontal cortex. This region is responsible for executive functions such as decision-making, self-regulation, and social perception. Charismatic individuals demonstrate enhanced activation and connectivity within the prefrontal cortex, enabling them to navigate social situations with ease, make persuasive arguments, and read social cues accurately.

Additionally, the limbic system, which governs emotions and motivations, contributes significantly to charisma. Charismatic individuals exhibit heightened activation in the amygdala, a key structure within the limbic system that processes emotions and detects social signals. This heightened emotional sensitivity allows charismatic individuals to establish a genuine connection with others, express empathy, and create an atmosphere of trust. Furthermore, the release of certain neurotransmitters, such as dopamine and oxytocin, is associated with charismatic behavior. Dopamine, known as the "feel-good" neurotransmitter, is linked to motivation, reward, and pleasure. Charismatic individuals experience an increase in dopamine levels, which fuels their confidence and enthusiasm. Oxytocin, often referred to as the "bonding hormone," is released during positive social interactions and fosters feelings of trust and connection. Charismatic individuals naturally trigger the release of oxytocin in others, establishing a deep sense of rapport and affiliation.

Beyond the realm of neuroscience, the study of evolutionary psychology sheds light on the origins and adaptive advantages of charisma. Throughout human history, charisma has served as an evolutionary advantage, enabling individuals to establish alliances, form social bonds, and navigate complex social hierarchies. Charismatic individuals were more likely to gain the support of their community, attract mates, and pass on their genes to future generations. Evolutionary psychologists propose that charisma signals high social status and resourcefulness, making charismatic individuals attractive both as allies and potential partners. This attractiveness stems from various factors, including displays of confidence, assertiveness, and social intelligence. Charismatic individuals exhibit behaviors that are evolutionarily advantageous, such as effective communication, empathy, and the ability to influence others. These qualities have been honed over generations, shaping our social instincts and responses.

Understanding the science behind charisma not only demystifies its allure but also empowers you to cultivate and enhance your own charismatic presence. By harnessing the knowledge of the neural processes and evolutionary underpinnings, you can develop strategies to boost your charisma and engage others more effectively. In the subsequent chapters of this book, we will explore practical techniques to tap into the neurological and evolutionary aspects of charisma. We will provide exercises to strengthen your social cognition, regulate your emotions, and refine your communication skills. By applying these insights and strategies, you will elevate your charismatic influence, forge deeper connections, and achieve greater success in your personal and professional endeavors.

Prepare to embark on an enlightening journey into the fascinating science of charisma. As we delve into the neural pathways, brain regions, neurotransmitters, and evolutionary roots, you will gain a comprehensive understanding of why charisma holds such profound influence over our social interactions. Armed with this knowledge, you will be equipped to unleash the power of charisma in your own life, fostering meaningful connections, and making a lasting impact on those around you.

CHAPTER 3

THE BENEFITS OF BEING CHARISMATIC: WHY BEING CHARISMATIC CAN BE BENEFICIAL FOR YOUR HEALTH AND WELLBEING

Charisma is not just a social asset; it has profound effects on our health, happiness, and overall wellbeing. In this chapter, we explore the remarkable benefits of being charismatic and how it can enhance various aspects of our lives. By understanding the positive impacts charisma can have on our mental and physical health, personal relationships, and professional success, you will be motivated to develop and cultivate your own charismatic qualities. Prepare to unlock the transformative power of charisma and embark on a journey towards a more fulfilling and rewarding life.

Enhanced Mental Health:

Charismatic individuals often experience significantly improved mental health outcomes. The ability to connect with others effortlessly, express oneself confidently, and establish deep and meaningful relationships contributes to a greater sense of belonging, purpose, and fulfillment. Charisma fosters a positive emotional state, promoting feelings of joy, enthusiasm, and optimism, which can counteract the negative effects of stress, anxiety, and depression. By actively developing and nurturing your charisma, you can cultivate a resilient mindset, build emotional well-being, and experience improved overall mental health and psychological well-being.

The impact of charisma on mental health is profound. Charismatic individuals possess exceptional social skills that allow them to navigate various social situations with ease. They are adept at engaging others in meaningful conversations, expressing themselves effectively, and creating connections that go beyond surface-level interactions. These skills not only enhance their social relationships but also contribute to their mental well-being. One of the key factors that contribute to enhanced mental health among charismatic individuals is a sense of belonging. Through their charismatic qualities, they create an inclusive and welcoming environment where others feel accepted and valued. This sense of belonging promotes a positive self-image and a greater sense of purpose, leading to improved overall mental well-being.

Charismatic individuals also possess a natural ability to foster positive emotions in themselves and others. Their optimistic outlook, enthusiasm, and zest for life can be infectious, spreading positivity and happiness to those around them. By cultivating charisma, individuals can tap into these positive emotions more readily, which can serve as a powerful buffer against stress, anxiety, and depression. Moreover, charisma enables individuals to build and maintain deep and meaningful relationships. These connections provide emotional support, a sense of security, and a source of validation. Charismatic individuals are skilled at active listening, empathizing with others, and offering genuine support. This not only strengthens their relationships but also contributes to their own emotional well-being.

Charismatic individuals also tend to have a strong sense of self-esteem and self-confidence. They are comfortable expressing themselves authentically, which fosters a positive self-image and reduces self-doubt. This confidence extends to their interactions with others, enabling them to navigate social situations with ease and assert themselves when necessary. By developing charisma, individuals can enhance their self-esteem and overall mental resilience. Additionally, charisma promotes a growth mindset and a sense of purpose. Charismatic individuals are often driven by a desire to make a positive impact on the world around them. They have a clear sense of purpose and strive to create meaningful connections and contribute to the well-being of others. This sense of purpose provides a sense of fulfillment and adds meaning to their lives, leading to improved mental health outcomes.

Improved Social Relationships:

Charismatic individuals excel in building and maintaining strong social connections. They possess exceptional communication skills, actively listen to others, and genuinely show interest in their perspectives and experiences. These qualities create a positive and inviting social environment, leading to the formation of deeper, more meaningful relationships. Charisma enables individuals to effortlessly establish rapport, earn trust, and foster lasting bonds with others. As a result, charismatic individuals enjoy a robust support network, experience heightened social satisfaction, and gain access to diverse perspectives and opportunities for personal and professional growth.

One of the most significant benefits of charisma lies in its ability to enhance social relationships. Charismatic individuals possess outstanding communication skills that enable them to express themselves effectively and engage others in meaningful conversations. They are skilled at active listening, paying close attention to others' thoughts and feelings, and responding with empathy and understanding. By demonstrating genuine interest and attentiveness, charismatic individuals create an environment where others feel valued, heard, and respected. The ability to establish rapport is another hallmark of charisma. Charismatic individuals have a natural charm that draws people to them. They can quickly establish connections with others, creating a sense of familiarity and comfort. Whether it's in a social gathering, a professional setting, or a casual encounter, charismatic individuals have a way of making others feel at ease and appreciated. This skill is invaluable in forming new relationships and expanding one's social network.

Trust is a vital element in any relationship, and charisma plays a significant role in earning and maintaining trust. Charismatic individuals exude authenticity and integrity, which inspires confidence and trust in others. Their ability to connect on a deeper level and demonstrate genuine care and empathy fosters trust and strengthens the bonds they form with others. As a result, they enjoy the loyalty and support of their social circle, enhancing their overall social satisfaction and well-being. Moreover, charisma opens doors to diverse perspectives and opportunities. Charismatic individuals attract a wide range of people from different backgrounds and experiences. This exposure to diverse perspectives and ideas broadens their own understanding of the world and provides opportunities for personal and professional growth. They can tap into the collective wisdom and knowledge of their social connections, gaining insights and fresh perspectives that enrich their lives.

Charismatic individuals also benefit from a robust support network. Their ability to build strong relationships means that they have a network of friends, mentors, and colleagues who can offer guidance, support, and encouragement. This support system is invaluable during challenging times, providing emotional assistance and practical help when needed. The sense of belonging and connection that comes from having a supportive network contributes to their overall well-being and resilience.

Improved Social Relationships:

Charismatic individuals excel in building and maintaining strong social connections. They possess exceptional communication skills, actively listen to others, and genuinely show interest in their perspectives and experiences. These qualities create a positive and inviting social environment, leading to the formation of deeper, more meaningful relationships. Charisma enables individuals to effortlessly establish rapport, earn trust, and foster lasting bonds with others. As a result, charismatic individuals enjoy a robust support network, experience heightened social satisfaction, and gain access to diverse perspectives and opportunities for personal and professional growth.

One of the key benefits of charisma is its ability to enhance social relationships. Charismatic individuals possess excellent communication skills, allowing them to express themselves effectively and engage others in meaningful conversations. They are adept at active listening, paying attention to others' thoughts and feelings, and responding empathetically. By demonstrating genuine interest and understanding, charismatic individuals create an environment where others feel valued, heard, and respected. The ability to establish rapport is another hallmark of charisma. Charismatic individuals have a natural charm that draws people to them. They can quickly build connections with others and create a sense of familiarity and comfort. Whether it's in a social gathering, a professional setting, or a casual encounter, charismatic individuals have a way of making others feel at ease and appreciated. This skill is invaluable in forming new relationships and expanding one's social network.

Trust is a crucial element in any relationship, and charisma plays a significant role in earning and maintaining trust. Charismatic individuals exude authenticity and integrity, which inspires confidence and trust in others. Their ability to connect on a deeper level and demonstrate genuine care and empathy fosters trust and strengthens the bonds they form with others. As a result, they enjoy the loyalty and support of their social circle, enhancing their overall social satisfaction and well-being. Moreover, charisma opens doors to diverse perspectives and opportunities. Charismatic individuals attract a wide range of people from different backgrounds and experiences. This exposure to diverse perspectives and ideas broadens their own understanding of the world and provides opportunities for personal and professional growth. They can tap into the collective wisdom and knowledge of their social connections, gaining insights and fresh perspectives that enrich their lives.

Charismatic individuals also benefit from a robust support network. Their ability to build strong relationships means that they have a network of friends, mentors, and colleagues who can offer guidance, support, and encouragement. This support system is invaluable during challenging times, providing emotional assistance and practical help when needed. The sense of belonging and connection that comes from having a supportive network contributes to their overall well-being and resilience.

Increased Persuasion and Influence:

Charismatic individuals possess a remarkable and enviable ability to persuade and influence others. With their magnetic presence, confident communication style, and genuine empathy, they have the power to sway opinions, gain support for their ideas, and mobilize people towards a common goal. Whether in personal relationships or professional environments, charisma empowers individuals to be highly persuasive communicators, enabling them to negotiate effectively, resolve conflicts amicably, and skillfully advocate for their needs and aspirations.

The persuasive impact of charisma lies in its multifaceted nature. Charismatic individuals possess a deep understanding of human psychology, enabling them to connect with others on an emotional level and tailor their messages accordingly. They have a keen sense of empathy, allowing them to comprehend the needs, desires, and concerns of those they seek to influence. By genuinely acknowledging and addressing these factors, charismatic individuals can craft their arguments and proposals in a manner that resonates deeply with their audience. Moreover, charisma is closely intertwined with effective storytelling. Charismatic individuals possess the art of captivating their listeners through compelling narratives, vivid descriptions, and engaging anecdotes. By weaving a captivating story, they can effectively convey their ideas and values, evoking emotions and stirring the imagination of their audience. This skillful storytelling not only captures attention but also leaves a lasting impact, making the message more memorable and influencing the listener's perception and decision-making process.

Charisma also empowers individuals to master the art of persuasion through nonverbal cues and body language. Charismatic individuals exude confidence, maintaining open and inviting postures, making eye contact, and utilizing expressive gestures. These nonverbal signals enhance their credibility, trustworthiness, and authenticity, ultimately strengthening their persuasive abilities. By aligning their verbal and nonverbal communication, charismatic individuals establish a sense of congruence and authenticity that resonates with their audience, fostering trust and receptiveness to their ideas. Furthermore, charismatic individuals possess exceptional interpersonal skills, allowing them to build rapport and establish genuine connections with others. They actively listen to others, demonstrating a genuine interest in their perspectives and experiences. This active listening fosters a sense of validation and respect, making others feel valued and understood. By valuing the opinions and contributions of others, charismatic individuals create a collaborative and inclusive environment, strengthening their persuasive influence.

Career Advancement:

The benefits of charisma extend far into the professional realm, offering charismatic individuals a significant advantage in terms of career success and advancement opportunities. Possessing the ability to build rapport, network effectively, and inspire trust, charismatic individuals find themselves at the forefront of new collaborations, promotions, and leadership roles. With charisma as their ally, they effortlessly navigate the complexities of the workplace, fostering positive relationships and creating an environment conducive to productivity and growth.

One of the key aspects that contribute to career advancement for charismatic individuals is their exceptional interpersonal skills. They have a natural ability to connect with colleagues, clients, and superiors, effortlessly establishing rapport and building relationships. Their genuine interest in others and adeptness at active listening create an atmosphere of trust and mutual respect, allowing for effective collaboration and teamwork. By fostering positive workplace relationships, charismatic individuals cultivate a supportive network that can propel their careers forward. Furthermore, charisma plays a pivotal role in effective communication within the professional setting. Charismatic individuals possess strong verbal and nonverbal communication skills, allowing them to express their thoughts and ideas with clarity and confidence. Their persuasive communication style enables them to articulate their vision, influence decision-making processes, and inspire others to act. This ability to communicate effectively and engage their colleagues and superiors makes them highly valued contributors in any organization.

Charisma also facilitates networking, a critical aspect of career advancement. Charismatic individuals possess the charm and social skills necessary to forge connections and build professional relationships with ease. They effortlessly navigate networking events, engaging others in meaningful conversations, and leaving a lasting impression. Their ability to make others feel comfortable and valued opens doors to new opportunities, whether it be collaborations, mentorships, or access to influential individuals in their field. In addition, charismatic individuals often find themselves in leadership positions, entrusted with greater responsibilities and decision-making authority. Their ability to inspire and motivate others, combined with their effective communication and interpersonal skills, makes them natural leaders. Charismatic leaders are adept at creating a positive work culture, fostering employee engagement and loyalty. Their ability to build and lead high-performing teams sets them apart and paves the way for continued career growth and success.

Moreover, charisma contributes to a positive and productive work environment. The magnetic presence and optimistic demeanor of charismatic individuals can uplift team morale and create a sense of enthusiasm and motivation. They excel at building a positive organizational culture where individuals feel valued, supported, and empowered to perform at their best. This positive work environment not only enhances job satisfaction but also attracts talented individuals, creating a reputation that can further propel their career trajectory.

Improved Wellbeing:

Being charismatic goes beyond social interactions; it has a profound impact on overall wellbeing and life satisfaction. The positive effects of charisma extend to various aspects of one's life, contributing to higher levels of happiness, self-esteem, and subjective well-being. By cultivating charisma, individuals can create a more positive and harmonious social environment, leading to greater overall wellbeing.

One of the ways in which charisma enhances wellbeing is through positive social interactions. Charismatic individuals excel at connecting with others, fostering a sense of belonging and inclusion. Their ability to engage in meaningful conversations, express empathy, and demonstrate genuine interest in others creates a positive social environment. These interactions provide emotional support, companionship, and a sense of community, which are essential for overall wellbeing. Research has shown that individuals with strong social connections experience lower levels of stress, improved mental health, and increased life satisfaction. Moreover, charisma plays a significant role in the development of meaningful relationships. charismatic individuals have the skills and qualities necessary to build deep and authentic connections. They are adept at active listening, demonstrating empathy, and understanding the needs of others. These qualities create a foundation of trust and intimacy, allowing for the formation of close friendships and romantic relationships. Meaningful relationships are essential for overall wellbeing as they provide emotional support, companionship, and a sense of purpose and fulfillment.

In addition to enhancing social interactions and relationships, charisma contributes to higher levels of happiness and self-esteem. Charismatic individuals often exude a positive and optimistic energy that is contagious. Their ability to inspire and uplift others creates a ripple effect, leading to increased happiness and positivity in their social circles. Furthermore, charisma boosts self-esteem as individuals feels confident in their ability to connect with others, express themselves effectively, and make a positive impact. This sense of self-assurance and positive self-perception contributes to overall wellbeing and a greater sense of fulfillment in life. Charismatic individuals also tend to have a greater sense of purpose and meaning in their lives. Their ability to inspire and motivate others allows them to make a positive difference in the lives of those around them. By leveraging their charisma, they can lead and influence others, working towards shared goals and causes. This sense of purpose and contribution to something larger than oneself enhances overall wellbeing and provides a sense of fulfillment and satisfaction.

Furthermore, charisma contributes to personal growth and self-actualization. Charismatic individuals are often open to new experiences and willing to step out of their comfort zones. They embrace challenges, take risks, and seize opportunities for growth. This mindset of continuous personal development fosters a sense of progress and accomplishment, leading to increased life satisfaction and overall wellbeing.

Reduced Stress and Improved Health:

The benefits of charisma extend beyond social interactions and have a positive impact on our physical health. Research has shown that individuals with strong social connections and positive social support systems tend to experience lower levels of stress, a reduced risk of cardiovascular diseases, and improved immune system function. The ability to connect with others and manage interpersonal relationships effect-tively, which is a hallmark of charisma, contributes to a healthier and more balanced life.

One of the ways in which charisma can improve health is by reducing stress levels. Charismatic individuals often possess excellent communication skills and a genuine interest in others, which allows them to build and maintain strong social connections. These connections provide emotional support, a sense of belonging, and opportunities for relaxation and recreation. When faced with challenging situations or stressors, having a strong social support system can help buffer the negative effects of stress. Charismatic individuals are more likely to have friends, family, or colleagues they can turn to for support, which can alleviate stress and promote overall well-being. Furthermore, charisma contributes to better cardiovascular health. Chronic stress is known to have detrimental effects on the cardiovascular system, increasing the risk of heart disease and other related conditions. By fostering positive social connections and managing relationships effectively, charismatic individuals can reduce stress levels and create a supportive environment that promotes cardiovascular health. Research has shown that individuals with strong social support systems have lower blood pressure, healthier cholesterol levels, and a reduced risk of heart disease. The ability to connect with others and build meaningful relationships contributes to a healthier heart and overall cardiovascular well-being.

In addition, charisma can positively impact immune system function. Chronic stress weakens the immune system, making individuals more susceptible to infections and illnesses. However, individuals with strong social connections and positive social support tend to have more robust immune system function. Charismatic individuals, with their ability to connect with others and build supportive relationships, can experience improved immune system response. The emotional support and sense of belonging provided by social connections contribute to a healthier immune system, enabling the body to fight off infections and diseases more effectively. Moreover, charisma can indirectly influence healthy behaviors. Charismatic individuals often serve as role models for others, inspiring and motivating them to adopt healthier habits. Their positive energy, enthusiasm, and ability to communicate effectively can influence those around them to engage in healthier lifestyle choices. For example, a charismatic colleague who promotes a healthy work-life balance may inspire others to prioritize self-care and stress management. By encouraging positive health behaviors, charismatic individuals contribute to the well-being of not only themselves but also those within their social circles.

Embracing charisma as a way of being can transform your life in remarkable ways. By developing your communication skills, empathy, and self-confidence, you can unlock the potential within you to become a more charismatic individual. As you embark on this journey, remember that charisma is not about being someone you're not, but rather about amplifying your authentic self and connecting with others in a meaningful way. In the upcoming chapters, we will delve deeper into practical strategies and techniques to cultivate and enhance your charisma. Get ready to unleash your charismatic potential and experience the multitude of benefits it brings to your health, relationships, and overall wellbeing.

CHAPTER 4

THE DARK SIDE OF CHARISMA: HOW CHARISMA CAN BE USED FOR MANIPULATION AND CONTROL

Charisma, with its captivating allure and influential power, has a darker side that must be acknowledged. In this chapter, we confront the uncomfortable truth that charisma can be used as a tool for manipulation and control. By exploring the tactics employed by individuals who misuse their charismatic abilities, we shed light on the warning signs and equip you with the necessary knowledge to protect yourself from potential harm. Furthermore, we delve into the ethical considerations surrounding charisma and emphasize the importance of using this gift responsibly and ethically.

Charm as a Mask:

Charismatic individuals who engage in manipulative behaviors often employ their charm as a deceptive mask to conceal their true intentions. They skillfully present themselves as caring, trustworthy, and empathetic, enticing others with their charismatic presence. However, behind this captivating facade, lies a darker reality: these individuals may harbor ulterior motives, seeking personal gain or power at the expense of others. Their charm becomes a tool for manipulation, allowing them to exploit unsuspecting individuals and manipulate situations to their advantage.

Exploiting Emotional Vulnerabilities:

Manipulative individuals with charisma possess a deep understanding of human emotions and vulnerabilities. They leverage their charm to exploit the insecurities and weaknesses of others, manipulating their emotions for their own benefit. By capitalizing on emotional vulnerabilities, they exert control and influence over their targets, creating an imbalanced power dynamic. Through calculated tactics and manipulation, they manipulate others into complying with their desires, furthering their own agenda while disregarding the well-being and autonomy of those they exploit.

Masterful Persuasion:

Charismatic manipulators possess exceptional skills in the art of persuasion. They have a remarkable ability to influence and convince others to adopt their viewpoints, make decisions in their favor, or engage in actions that serve their interests. Through their eloquent speech, compelling arguments, confident body language, and a deep understanding of human psychology, they can effectively sway opinions, override critical thinking, and manipulate the thought processes of their targets. Their mastery of persuasive techniques allows them to exert control and manipulate situations to align with their desired outcomes.

Creating a Cult of Personality:

In the most extreme cases, charismatic individuals with manipulative tendencies may establish a cult-like following around themselves. Through the potent combination of their charm, charisma, and manipulative tactics, they create an environment where a sense of devotion and unwavering loyalty is fostered among their followers. They cultivate an aura of authority and superiority, often presenting themselves as exceptional or even divine beings. In this toxic dynamic, dissenting voices are silenced, critical thinking is discouraged, and blind obedience is demanded. The followers may be made to believe in the manipulator's infallibility, reinforcing the power imbalance and perpetuating the cycle of manipulation and control.

Isolating and Controlling Others:

Manipulative individuals adeptly use their charisma to isolate their targets from external influences and support networks. They strategically create a sense of dependency, where the targets become increasingly reliant on their approval, companionship, or guidance. Through their charm and manipulation, they gradually erode relationships with friends, family, and other sources of support, leaving the targets feeling isolated and vulnerable. By isolating their victims, manipulators gain greater control over their thoughts, actions, and emotions.

Gaslighting and Emotional Manipulation:

Charismatic manipulators possess a deep under-standing of emotional manipulation techniques, including the insidious practice of gaslighting. They skillfully distort reality, undermine the perceptions and memories of their targets, and create a pervasive sense of doubt and confusion. Gaslighting can lead the targets to question their own sanity, judgment, and reality. Through this psychological manipulation, the manipulator gains power and control over the emotions, thoughts, and behaviors of their victims. Gaslighting erodes the targets' self-confidence, creates a reliance on the manipulator for validation and guidance, and perpetuates the cycle of manipulation and control.

Leveraging Charisma for Personal Gain:

Charismatic manipulators frequently prioritize their own self-interests above the well-being of others. They skillfully utilize their charm, influence, and persuasive abilities to exploit various situations, acquire resources, or gain advantages at the expense of those around them. Their charisma becomes a strategic tool for personal enrichment, enabling them to accumulate power, control, and material benefits while disregarding the impact on others. Through their manipulative tactics, they capitalize on opportunities for personal gain, often leaving a trail of disillusionment and harm in their wake.

It is crucial to recognize and protect yourself from the manipulative tendencies that can accompany charisma. Here are some strategies to safeguard against manipulation:

- Develop Awareness: Educate yourself about the tactics employed by manipulative individuals. Learn to recognize the warning signs of manipulation, such as excessive flattery, inconsistencies in their words and actions, and attempts to isolate or control you.

- Trust Your Intuition: Pay attention to your gut feelings and instincts. If something feels off or you sense that someone is trying to manipulate you, trust your intuition and take necessary precautions.

- Establish Healthy Boundaries: Set clear boundaries and assert yourself when necessary. Manipulative individuals may try to push your limits and exploit your willingness to please. By establishing and enforcing healthy boundaries, you protect yourself from undue influence.

- Seek Support: Build a strong support network of trusted friends, family, or mentors who can provide guidance and objective perspectives. They can offer valuable insights and support if you find yourself in a potentially manipulative situation.

- Practice Critical Thinking: Develop your critical thinking skills to evaluate information objectively. Question assumptions, seek evidence, and consider alternative perspectives before making decisions or accepting someone's claims.

It is important to emphasize that charisma itself is not inherently negative; rather, it is the intent and actions of individuals that determine its impact. By recognizing the dark side of charisma and being aware of manipulative tactics, we can use our own charisma responsibly, fostering positive connections and creating a supportive social environment.

In the following chapters, we will explore how to cultivate authentic charisma that aligns with ethical principles, allowing you to harness its positive power while avoiding its pitfalls.

CHAPTER 5

HOW TO BE CHARISMATIC: TIPS AND ADVICE FOR BECOMING MORE LIKEABLE AND SOCIABLE

Charisma is not an innate trait reserved for a select few; it can be developed and nurtured through conscious effort and practice. In this chapter, we provide you with practical tips and actionable advice to help you enhance your charisma and become more likeable and sociable. Whether you're an introvert looking to step out of your comfort zone or simply seeking to improve your social skills, these strategies will empower you to make meaningful connections and leave a lasting impression on others.

Authenticity and Self-Awareness:

Embrace your true self and cultivate self-awareness. Authenticity forms the bedrock of charisma. It is essential to recognize and embrace your strengths, values, and passions, allowing them to shine through in your interactions. When you are authentic and genuine, others are naturally drawn to your sincerity and unique qualities. By cultivating self-awareness, you can develop a deeper understanding of yourself, including your emotions, motivations, and behavior patterns. This self-awareness enables you to align your actions with your true self, fostering a sense of congruence and authenticity in your interactions with others. Embracing authenticity and nurturing self-awareness are key steps toward developing and enhancing your charisma.

Positive Body Language:

Your body language speaks volumes even before you utter a word. It is a powerful tool for projecting confidence and creating a positive impression. By paying attention to your body language, you can enhance your charisma and connect more effectively with others. Start by maintaining good posture, standing tall with your shoulders relaxed and your head held high. This posture conveys confidence and openness, inviting others to engage with you. Make eye contact with others, as it signals attentiveness and engagement, establishing a sense of connection. When engaging in conversations, use open gestures, such as open palms and expansive arm movements, to create a sense of openness and receptiveness. Additionally, remember to smile genuinely, as it radiates warmth and approachability, making others feel comfortable and at ease in your presence. By being mindful of your facial expressions and body positioning, you can convey a sense of authenticity, openness, and positivity, enhancing your charisma and creating a favorable impression on others.

Active Listening:

Being a good listener is a crucial component of developing charisma. It involves demonstrating genuine interest in others by actively engaging in the listening process. When someone is speaking, make a conscious effort to maintain eye contact, nod in acknowledgment, and provide verbal and non-verbal cues that indicate your engagement. Show curiosity and ask follow-up questions to delve deeper into their thoughts and experiences. By giving others the space to express themselves and truly listening to what they have to say, you create a positive and supportive environment that fosters meaningful connections.

Empathy and Emotional Intelligence:

Cultivating empathy and emotional intelligence is vital for building strong connections and deepening your charisma. Empathy involves putting yourself in someone else's shoes and seeking to understand their perspectives, emotions, and experiences. Show compassion and validate their feelings, demonstrating that you genuinely care about their well-being. Developing emotional intelligence allows you to recognize and understand your own emotions and those of others, enabling you to navigate social interactions with sensitivity and insight. By cultivating empathy and emotional intelligence, you can establish a deeper level of connection and trust, enhancing your charisma and creating meaningful relationships.

Engaging Conversation:

Mastering the art of engaging conversation is a skill that enhances your charisma and strengthens your connections with others. It involves focusing on meaningful topics and actively participating in discussions. Show genuine curiosity about others' experiences, opinions, and interests, and ask open-ended questions that invite them to share more. By showing a sincere interest in what others have to say, you create an atmosphere of respect and validation. Additionally, share your own stories and experiences, allowing others to relate to you on a personal level. Engaging in authentic and meaningful conversations fosters a sense of connection, fosters rapport, and enhances your charisma in social interactions.

Confidence and Assertiveness:

Developing confidence in expressing your thoughts and ideas is a vital aspect of charisma. It entails cultivating a deep belief in yourself and your abilities, allowing you to project a sense of assurance and conviction. By practicing assertiveness, you can respectfully voice your opinions and stand up for yourself when necessary. The embodiment of confidence and assertiveness demonstrates strength, self-assuredness, and determination, which can be highly appealing to others and command their attention and respect.

Sense of Humor:

Cultivating a well-rounded sense of humor is a powerful tool for enhancing your charisma. It involves developing the ability to find joy and amusement in everyday situations, allowing you to lighten the mood and create a positive and enjoyable atmosphere. By utilizing appropriate humor, you can effectively connect with others, foster camaraderie, and make yourself more approachable. A well-timed joke or witty remark can break the ice, relieve tension, and create a shared sense of laughter, ultimately strengthening social bonds and building rapport with others.

Adaptability and Flexibility:

Demonstrating adaptability and flexibility in your interactions is a crucial skill for nurturing charisma. By paying close attention to the social cues and dynamics of others, you can adeptly adjust your communication style to suit the needs of different individuals and situations. This ability showcases your willingness to understand and accommodate the preferences and perspectives of others, making you more relatable and inclusive. By remaining open-minded and adaptable, you can create a more harmonious and engaging social environment, fostering deeper connections and facilitating meaningful interactions with a diverse range of people.

Building Rapport:

Building rapport is a fundamental aspect of charismatic interactions. It involves establishing a connection and fostering a sense of understanding and trust with others. One effective way to build rapport is by finding common ground and shared interests. By actively listening and engaging in meaningful conversations, you can uncover shared passions and experiences that create a sense of familiarity and connection. Building rapport allows you to create a comfortable and harmonious atmosphere, making others more receptive to your presence and message.

Continuous Learning and Growth:

Embracing a mindset of continuous learning and growth is essential for enhancing your charisma. Committing to ongoing personal and professional development allows you to expand your knowledge, skills, and experiences, making you more interesting and engaging in conversations. Seek out opportunities to learn from various sources such as books, courses, workshops, and diverse perspectives. Embracing continuous learning not only enriches your own life but also enables you to contribute valuable insights and perspectives to conversations, making you a well-rounded and dynamic individual. By demonstrating a commitment to growth, you inspire others to pursue their own development and create a positive and intellectually stimulating social environment.

Remember, developing charisma is a journey that requires time, effort, and practice. It's important to be patient with yourself and acknowledge the progress you make along the way, no matter how small. Embrace opportunities to step outside of your comfort zone and actively engage in social interactions that push your boundaries. By challenging yourself and continuously learning and growing, you can cultivate a magnetic presence that naturally attracts others. In the upcoming chapters, we will delve deeper into specific techniques and exercises that will further enhance your charisma and elevate your social interactions. These tools will equip you with practical strategies to enhance your communication skills, strengthen your emotional intelligence, and deepen your connections with others. Through dedicated practice and a commitment to self-improvement, you will become more confident, influential, and engaging in social settings. Stay curious and open-minded as you explore the various techniques and exercises. Be willing to experiment and adapt them to suit your unique personality and style. Remember, charisma is not about imitating someone else, but rather about authentically expressing yourself in a way that resonates with others.

As you continue this journey, keep in mind that building charisma is not just about external charm, but also about developing inner qualities such as empathy, authenticity, and self-awareness. By nurturing these qualities alongside the external techniques, you will create a solid foundation for long-lasting and meaningful connections. So, let's embark on this exciting journey together, as we uncover the secrets to unlocking your full charismatic potential. Get ready to discover new insights, sharpen your skills, and transform your social interactions for the better.

CHAPTER 6

HOW TO USE YOUR CHARISMA: HOW TO BE MORE PERSUASIVE AND INFLUENTIAL

Charismatic individuals possess a unique ability to persuade and influence others. In this chapter, we delve into the techniques and strategies that can enhance your persuasive power and elevate your influence. By mastering the art of charisma, you'll be able to captivate audiences, sway opinions, and inspire positive action. Whether you're looking to excel in your professional life, engage in effective leadership, or simply make a meaningful impact, the following tips and strategies will guide you towards becoming a more persuasive and influential individual.

Storytelling Mastery:

The power of storytelling cannot be underestimated. Charismatic individuals possess a remarkable ability to captivate and engage their audience through masterful storytelling. They skillfully weave personal experiences, emotions, and vivid imagery into their narratives, creating a deep and meaningful connection with their listeners. By leveraging the art of storytelling, you can harness the emotional impact of your stories to resonate with others on a profound level. Craft your stories with authenticity, incorporating relatable themes and compelling plotlines that evoke emotions and leave a lasting impression.

Persuasive Language:

Words have the potential to influence and inspire action. Charismatic individuals understand the art of persuasive language and carefully select their words to convey their ideas with impact. They employ rhetorical techniques such as repetition, metaphors, and powerful imagery to emphasize key points and leave a lasting imprint on their audience's minds. By mastering the art of persuasive language, you can craft your messages in a way that resonates deeply with your listeners, addressing their values and aspirations. Pay attention to the tone, cadence, and delivery of your words, ensuring they align with your audience's preferences and desires.

Active Listening and Empathy:

Persuasion is not solely about speaking; it also involves understanding and connecting with others. Charismatic individuals recognize the importance of active listening and empathy in building meaningful relationships and influencing others. They practice the art of truly hearing and understanding their audience's needs, desires, and concerns. By actively listening and demonstrating genuine empathy, you establish a foundation of trust and rapport, making others more receptive to your ideas and suggestions. Cultivate your active listening skills, allowing others to feel heard and valued. Show genuine empathy by putting yourself in their shoes, acknowledging their emotions, and responding with understanding and compassion.

Building Credibility and Trust:

Charismatic individuals are not only captivating speakers but also seen as trustworthy and credible sources of information. To enhance your credibility, focus on showcasing your expertise, credentials, and past successes in a genuine and humble manner. Provide concrete evidence, statistics, and relevant examples to back up your claims. By establishing yourself as knowledgeable and reliable, you build trust with your audience, making them more receptive to your persuasive efforts.

Charismatic Body Language:

Nonverbal communication speaks volumes in persuasion. Pay close attention to your body language as it can significantly impact how your message is received. Project confidence by maintaining an upright posture, using open gestures, and purposeful movements. Maintain eye contact to establish a connection and convey sincerity. Be mindful of your facial expressions, ensuring they align with your intended message. A warm and engaging smile can go a long way in building rapport and making others feel at ease.

Adaptability and Flexibility:

Effective persuasion requires the ability to adapt and be flexible in your approach. Recognize that different individuals and situations call for varied communication styles. Tailor your tone, language, and arguments to resonate with the preferences and values of your audience. Show empathy by understanding their unique perspectives and adapting your message to address their specific needs. By demonstrating your willingness to listen and adjust, you increase the likelihood of influencing their opinions and decisions.

Creating a Vision:

Charismatic individuals not only possess a compelling presence but also have a clear vision for the future. Take the time to develop a captivating vision that ignites enthusiasm and inspires others to act. Articulate the benefits and positive outcomes of embracing your vision, highlighting how individuals can contribute and be part of the transformative journey. By painting a vivid picture of the future, you create a sense of purpose and motivation that resonates with others.

Confidence and Charismatic Presence:

Confidence is a fundamental aspect of charisma. Cultivate a strong sense of self-assurance, belief in your ideas, and conviction in your abilities. Project charisma through your presence, commanding attention, and respect. Hold yourself with poise and maintain a calm demeanor, even in challenging situations. When you exude confidence, others are more likely to trust your judgment and follow your lead.

Ethical Influence:

As a charismatic individual, it is crucial to use your persuasive skills in an ethical and responsible manner. Consider the impact of your influence on others and ensure that your intentions are aligned with ethical principles. Use persuasion as a tool for creating positive change, empowering others, and fostering collaboration. Strive to build genuine connections and engage in transparent and respectful communication. By using your charisma ethically, you can create a lasting impact and inspire others to achieve their full potential.

Practice and Feedback:

Developing persuasive skills and leveraging charisma for positive impact requires consistent practice. Actively seek out opportunities to apply your persuasive techniques in different settings, such as presentations, discussions, or negotiations. Embrace challenges and learn from each experience to enhance your abilities. Additionally, seek feedback from trusted individuals who can provide valuable insights and constructive criticism. Their feedback will help you identify areas for improvement and refine your approach. By dedicating yourself to continuous practice and seeking feedback, you can strengthen your persuasive abilities and maximize the positive impact of your charisma.

By mastering the techniques and strategies outlined in this chapter, you will enhance your persuasive abilities and become a more influential individual. The art of persuasion is a powerful tool that can positively impact your personal and professional life. In the next chapter, we will delve into the intricacies of building solid relationships and deepening connections through the application of charm and charisma. Building strong relationships is essential for success and fulfillment in various aspects of life.

Whether it's establishing rapport with colleagues, connecting with clients, or fostering meaningful friendships, charm and charisma play a significant role in creating lasting bonds. We will explore the key principles and practices that can help you cultivate and nurture these relationships.

Throughout the chapter, we will discuss the importance of empathy and understanding, as well as the power of authenticity and genuine interest. We will also delve into the significance of positive attitude and optimism, the role of humor in building rapport, and the impact of kindness and thoughtfulness on relationship dynamics. Effective communication, shared experiences, and empowering others will also be key areas of focus. Furthermore, we will delve into the ethical aspect of influence, emphasizing the importance of using your charisma and persuasive skills responsibly and ethically. We will explore how you can influence others in a positive and empowering way, creating a ripple effect of positive change.

Additionally, we will touch upon the significance of continuous growth, highlighting the value of practice and seeking feedback for honing your persuasive techniques. By continuously refining your skills, you will become more adept at leveraging your charisma for positive impact. As we progress through the chapter, you will gain a deeper understanding of the multifaceted nature of building solid relationships through charm and charisma. You will be equipped with practical strategies and insights that will enable you to foster connections, inspire action, and create a positive impact on those around you.

So, get ready to unlock the secrets of building solid relationships and deepening connections through the art of charm and charisma. Together, we will explore the transformative power of these qualities and discover how they can enrich your personal and professional life.

CHAPTER 7

HOW TO BE MORE CHARMING: BUILDING SOLID RELATIONSHIPS

Charm is a powerful quality that can help you build strong and meaningful relationships with others. In this chapter, we explore the essence of charm and provide practical guidance on how to cultivate it in your interactions. By developing empathy, authenticity, and warmth, you can create connections that go beyond surface-level interactions. Let's delve into the art of being charming and discover how it can enhance your personal and professional relationships.

Empathy and Understanding: The Foundation of Strong Relationships

Developing and nurturing solid relationships hinges on the core values of empathy and understanding. It entails going beyond surface-level interactions and truly connecting with others on a deeper, more meaningful level. To cultivate empathy, it is crucial to develop a genuine desire to comprehend and appreciate the perspectives, emotions, and experiences of those around you. This involves stepping into their shoes, seeking to understand the world through their eyes, and acknowledging the uniqueness of their journey.

Empathy is not simply a passive acknowledgment of others' feelings; it requires active engagement and sincere interest in their lives. By actively listening to their stories, challenges, and triumphs, you convey a genuine concern and demonstrate that their thoughts and experiences matter. Engaging in meaningful conversations, free from judgment, allows you to gain insights into their values, aspirations, and fears. Through this process, you can establish a deeper connection and develop a more profound under-standing of their essence.

Actively practicing empathy also involves recognizing and validating the emotions experienced by others. By empathetically acknowledging their joys, sorrows, frustrations, and fears, you create a safe space for them to express themselves authentically.

This validation fosters a sense of trust, as individuals feel seen, heard, and understood. It reinforces the belief that their feelings and experiences are legitimate and worthy of consideration.

Furthermore, empathy extends beyond verbal communication. It encompasses nonverbal cues, such as body language and facial expressions, that convey a sense of genuine understanding and compassion. Being attentive to these cues allows you to connect on a deeper level, forging a bond that goes beyond words alone.

Ultimately, empathy and understanding lay the groundwork for meaningful relationships. They enable you to navigate the intricacies of human emotions, bridging gaps and fostering connections based on mutual respect, support, and appreciation. By cultivating empathy in your interactions, you contribute to a world where individuals feel valued, understood, and accepted—a world where relationships thrive on the bedrock of empathy and understanding.

Authenticity and Genuine Interest: The Power of Being Your True Self

Charm that stems from authenticity is a force that captivates and resonates with others. Embracing your true self is a powerful tool in cultivating genuine connections and exuding an irresistible charisma. It begins with recognizing and celebrating your unique qualities, strengths, and quirks—the aspects that make you who you are.

When you embrace your authenticity, you project an aura of self-assurance and confidence. You radiate an unmistakable energy that draws others in and invites them to explore the depths of your character. By being true to yourself, you send a message that you are comfortable in your own skin, which is both refreshing and captivating to those around you. In addition to embracing your authenticity, showing a genuine interest in others is essential for building meaningful connections. Instead of merely engaging in surface-level conversations, strive to dig deeper and truly understand the individuals you interact with. This genuine interest involves actively listening to their stories, perspectives, and experiences with an open heart and mind.

By asking thoughtful questions and attentively listening to their responses, you convey a sincere desire to connect and understand. Engaging in meaningful conversations allows you to unravel the layers of their personality and develop a deeper appreciation for their unique qualities. It signals to others that you value their thoughts and experiences, fostering a sense of trust and respect. Moreover, being present in the moment is a crucial aspect of displaying authenticity and genuine interest. When you are fully engaged in the conversation, your undivided attention speaks volumes. It shows that you value the time and space you share with others and that you are invested in the exchange.

Authenticity and genuine interest go hand in hand, creating a powerful synergy that underlies true charisma. When you are authentic, you become a magnet for others who appreciate your honesty and integrity. Your genuine interest in their lives and experiences fosters a deep sense of connection, allowing relationships to flourish and grow. In a world often marked by superficiality, embracing authenticity, and showing genuine interest are acts of rebellion. They invite others to embrace their own uniqueness and feel comfortable in their skin. By embodying these qualities, you become a catalyst for positive change, inspiring others to embrace their true selves and fostering a culture of authenticity and genuine connections.

Positive Attitude and Optimism: Harnessing the Power of Positivity

A positive attitude is a magnetic force that can amplify your charm and leave a lasting impression on those around you. It is a mindset that embraces the bright side of life, finding opportunities and silver linings even in challenging situations. Cultivating a positive attitude not only uplifts your own spirit but also radiates a contagious energy that draws others towards you.

Maintaining an optimistic outlook is key to fostering your charm. It involves consciously choosing to focus on the positive aspects of people, circumstances, and experiences. Instead of dwelling on setbacks or negativity, shift your perspective towards growth, learning, and the possibilities that lie ahead. This optimistic mindset allows you to approach challenges with resilience and determination, inspiring others with your unwavering belief in the power of optimism. One of the most effective ways to demonstrate a positive attitude is through enthusiasm. Let your passion and excitement shine through in your interactions. Show genuine interest and curiosity in the conversations you have, and express enthusiasm for the topics being discussed. Your enthusiasm is infectious, captivating the attention of those around you and making them feel energized and engaged.

A warm and genuine smile is a powerful tool in exuding positivity and charm. It is a universal language that communicates warmth, approachability, and friendliness. Smiling not only uplifts your own mood but also creates an inviting and welcoming atmosphere for others. When you genuinely smile, you make others feel comfortable and at ease in your presence, encouraging open and authentic connections. Maintaining a positive attitude and exuding optimism does not mean denying or suppressing negative emotions. It is about acknowledging and accepting challenges but choosing to approach them with a constructive and hopeful mindset. By acknowledging setbacks and difficulties while maintaining a positive outlook, you inspire others to do the same and contribute to a supportive and empowering environment.

In a world that can often be filled with negativity and uncertainty, a positive attitude becomes a beacon of hope and resilience. It attracts like-minded individuals who are drawn to your uplifting energy and outlook on life. Your positive disposition creates a ripple effect, inspiring others to embrace optimism and seek the silver linings in their own lives. So, embrace the power of positivity. Cultivate a positive attitude that radiates optimism, enthusiasm, and warmth. Through your genuine smiles, uplifting energy, and hopeful mindset, you become a charismatic force that brightens the lives of those around you, leaving a lasting impact and fostering connections rooted in positivity and joy.

Good Sense of Humor: Harnessing the Power of Laughter

A well-developed sense of humor is a delightful tool that can enhance your charm and create meaningful connections with others. It is the ability to find joy in everyday situations, share lighthearted moments, and bring laughter into the lives of those around you. Cultivating a good sense of humor involves appreciating wit, wordplay, and the nuances of comedic timing. One way to nurture your sense of humor is by immersing yourself in comedy and humor. Explore different genres of humor, such as observational comedy, satire, or situational humor.

Watch stand-up comedy shows, read humorous books, or engage with witty content that tickles your funny bone. By exposing yourself to various forms of humor, you can expand your comedic repertoire and develop your own unique comedic style.

Using humor in social interactions can create a light-hearted and enjoyable atmosphere. Find appropriate moments to share humorous anecdotes, clever remarks, or witty comebacks. A well-placed joke or a clever play on words cannot only bring a smile to people's faces but also ease tension and foster camaraderie. However, it is essential to be mindful of the context and the preferences of those around you. Respect boundaries and ensure that your humor is inclusive and sensitive to diverse perspectives. A good sense of humor is not just about making others laugh; it is also about being able to laugh at yourself. Embrace self-deprecating humor, which involves playfully acknowledging your own quirks and foibles. This demonstrates humility and authenticity, making you more relatable and endearing to others.

Humor has the power to transcend cultural and language barriers, forging connections and creating shared experiences. When you share a laugh with someone, it builds rapport and strengthens the bond between you. Laughter has been shown to reduce stress, foster positive emotions, and improve overall well-being. By infusing humor into your interactions, you contribute to a more joyful and uplifting environment. However, it is important to be mindful of the appropriateness of your jokes. Consider the context, the sensitivities of the people around you, and any potential impact your humor may have. Avoid jokes that may offend or hurt others and always prioritize creating a safe and inclusive space for everyone.

Kindness and Thoughtfulness: Nurturing Connections through Genuine Care

Kindness and thoughtfulness are powerful ingredients that contribute to your charm and the strength of your relationships. By embodying these qualities, you can create a positive and nurturing environment where others feel valued and appreciated. Acts of kindness, no matter how small, have the potential to leave a lasting impact on the hearts and minds of those around you. To cultivate kindness and thoughtfulness, start by being mindful of the needs and emotions of others. Take the time to listen attentively when someone shares their thoughts or concerns and respond with empathy and understanding. Show genuine interest in their lives, dreams, and aspirations. This demonstrates that you value their presence and that their well-being matters to you.

Offering compliments from a place of sincerity is another way to spread kindness. Take notice of people's strengths, achievements, or unique qualities, and express your appreciation for them. Whether it's a simple compliment on someone's style, a recognition of their hard work, or a heartfelt acknowledgment of their character, these words of affirmation can boost their confidence and foster a sense of connection. Acts of service and assistance are also meaningful ways to demonstrate kindness and thoughtfulness. Extend a helping hand when someone is in need, whether it's helping with a task, supporting them during challenging times, or simply lending an ear to listen. Your willingness to offer support and contribute to their well-being shows that you genuinely care.

Moreover, expressing gratitude is an important aspect of thoughtfulness. Take the time to acknowledge and appreciate the efforts and contributions of others. Show your gratitude through simple gestures like saying "thank you," writing a heartfelt note, or offering a small token of appreciation. By recognizing and valuing the positive impact that others have on your life, you foster a sense of connection and mutual respect. Kindness and thoughtfulness create a ripple effect. When you extend genuine care and consideration to others, it inspires them to do the same. This virtuous cycle of kindness strengthens relationships, builds trust, and enhances the overall well-being of the people around you.

In a world that can sometimes feel disconnected and impersonal, acts of kindness and thoughtfulness have the power to bridge gaps and bring people closer together. By making a conscious effort to infuse your interactions with kindness, you contribute to a more compassionate and harmonious social fabric. So, let kindness and thoughtfulness be the guiding principles in your quest for charm, and watch as the positive energy you create ripples out into the world.

Effective Communication: The Pathway to Meaningful Connections

Effective communication serves as a cornerstone for building strong and meaningful relationships. It is through clear and authentic expression that we connect with others on a deeper level. By honing your communication skills, you can create an environment of openness, understanding, and trust. To communicate effectively, start by expressing your thoughts and feelings honestly and respectfully. Be genuine in your words and convey your ideas with clarity. Speak in a manner that is both assertive and considerate, sharing your perspective while also being receptive to the viewpoints of others. By fostering an atmosphere of mutual respect, you encourage open dialogue and create space for meaningful conversations.

Nonverbal communication plays a significant role in effective communication as well. Pay attention to your body language and facial expressions, as they can convey messages that are just as powerful as words. Maintain eye contact to demonstrate attentiveness and interest in the conversation. Use open and welcoming gestures to invite others to share their thoughts and feelings. Nodding and other affirming gestures can show understanding and encourage the speaker to continue expressing themselves. Equally important in effective communication is the art of active listening. Give your full attention to the person speaking, setting aside distractions, and truly engaging in the conversation. Practice empathy by putting yourself in their shoes and seeking to understand their perspectives and emotions. Show that you are actively listening by paraphrasing their statements, asking clarifying questions, and providing meaningful feedback. By demonstrating that you value and respect their input, you foster a sense of connection and encourage further dialogue.

Validation is another crucial aspect of effective communication. Acknowledge and validate the perspectives and feelings of others, even if you may not fully agree with them. By affirming their experiences and emotions, you create a safe and non-judgmental space for open communication. This validation helps build trust and encourages individuals to share more openly, fostering deeper connections.

Shared Experiences: Nurturing Bonds Through Meaningful Connections

Shared experiences hold a remarkable ability to forge and fortify relationships, as they create a shared tapestry of memories and emotions. By actively engaging in activities and conversations that foster a deeper connection, you can cultivate bonds that stand the test of time. Discovering common interests forms the foundation for creating shared experiences. Seek out activities or hobbies that ignite mutual enthusiasm and curiosity. It could be attending cultural events, exploring the outdoors, engaging in artistic endeavors, or embarking on adventures together. By participating in these shared activities, you embark on a journey of discovery, learning, and growth side by side.

Meaningful conversations also provide an avenue for shared experiences. Engage in deep and thought-provoking discussions that delve into personal beliefs, dreams, and aspirations. Share your experiences, values, and perspectives, while wholeheartedly embracing the stories and insights of others. By opening up and fostering vulnerability, you create a space for authentic connections to flourish. During these shared experiences, it is essential to be fully present and attentive. Immerse yourself in the moment, allowing the beauty and joy of the experience to unfold naturally. Listen actively to one another, exchanging thoughts, ideas, and emotions. Celebrate each other's accomplishments and support each other through challenges. By truly engaging in these shared moments, you solidify the bonds and create lasting memories.

The benefits of shared experiences extend beyond the present moment. The memories created together become a shared narrative, strengthening the connection between individuals. These memories serve as a wellspring of joy, nostalgia, and comfort, offering a unique bond that brings people closer even when physically apart. It is important to remember that shared experiences can take various forms and need not be extravagant or elaborate. Simple acts of kindness, such as cooking a meal together, taking a leisurely stroll, or engaging in a heartfelt conversation, can create profound connections. The key lies in the intention and the genuine desire to cultivate shared moments that enrich and deepen relationships.

In summary, shared experiences serve as a powerful catalyst for building and nurturing relationships. Through engaging in activities, pursuing common interests, and engaging in meaningful conversations, you create a tapestry of shared memories and emotions. Embrace the opportunity to embark on these journeys together, for they form the threads that weave unbreakable bonds of connection and understanding.

Empowering Others: Fostering Growth and Supportive Relationships

Charm holds a transformative power that extends beyond personal likability—it encompasses the ability to uplift and empower those around you. By actively encouraging and supporting others, you create a nurturing environment where individuals can thrive, and relationships can flourish. One of the fundamental ways to empower others is through the gift of words. Offer genuine and heartfelt words of affirmation, expressing appreciation for their unique qualities, talents, and contributions. Acknowledge their achievements, both big and small, and celebrate their successes. Your words of encouragement can ignite a spark of confidence and inspire them to reach greater heights.

In addition to words, provide tangible support whenever possible. Be attentive to the needs and challenges faced by those around you and offer a helping hand when they require assistance. Whether it's lending a listening ear, providing guidance, or collaborating on projects, your support can make a significant difference in their journey. By being a reliable source of support, you create an environment where individuals feel valued and empowered to overcome obstacles. Furthermore, create opportunities for growth and development. Encourage others to pursue their passions, explore new interests, and step outside their comfort zones. Offer guidance, resources, and connections that can help them unlock their full potential. By fostering an environment that embraces growth, you inspire others to discover their strengths, overcome limitations, and embrace new possibilities.

It is important to approach empowerment with authenticity and genuine intentions. Your actions should stem from a sincere desire to uplift others rather than seeking personal gain or control. Empowerment thrives in an environment of trust, respect, and empathy. By valuing and validating the unique perspectives, experiences, and aspirations of others, you create a safe space where they feel supported and encouraged to become their best selves.

Remember, empowering others is not a one-time act but a continuous commitment. It requires consistent effort, active listening, and a willingness to adapt to the evolving needs of those around you. By nurturing a culture of empowerment, you create a ripple effect, inspiring others to embrace their own power and uplift those around them. The collective growth and success that emerge from such an environment fosters deep and meaningful relationships built on mutual support and shared aspirations. In summary, charm goes beyond personal likability — it encompasses the ability to empower and uplift others. Through genuine words of affirmation, tangible support, and opportunities for growth, you create a nurturing environment that fosters personal development and flourishing relationships. By embracing the power to empower, you become a catalyst for positive change and inspire others to reach their highest potential.

Respect and Integrity: The Foundation of Lasting Charm

Charm is intricately woven with respect and integrity, forming the bedrock of meaningful connections. By treating others with genuine respect and embodying unwavering integrity, you cultivate an environment where charm can flourish.

Respect is the cornerstone of any healthy relationship. Embrace the diversity of individuals around you, recognizing their unique backgrounds, beliefs, and perspectives. Show kindness and consideration in your interactions, valuing each person's inherent worth. Listen attentively to their thoughts and opinions, even when you disagree. By embracing respect as a guiding principle, you create an atmosphere of acceptance and appreciation, fostering deeper connections. Integrity is the embodiment of honesty, trustworthiness, and consistency in your words and actions. Be true to your values and principles and let them guide your decisions and behaviors. Act with transparency, avoiding deception or manipulation. When your words align seamlessly with your deeds, you cultivate a sense of authenticity and reliability that others can rely on. Integrity forms the bedrock of trust, an essential component of charm.

To establish and uphold respect and integrity, it is crucial to approach interactions with empathy and humility. Seek to understand others' experiences and perspectives, even if they differ from your own. Embrace a growth mindset, recognizing that you have much to learn from others. Admit and learn from your mistakes and apologize sincerely when necessary. By demonstrating humility and a willingness to grow, you foster an environment of mutual respect and authenticity.

Furthermore, be mindful of the impact of your actions on others. Treat confidential information with utmost care and refrain from gossip or spreading rumors. Honor your commitments and follow through on your promises. When you consistently demonstrate reliability and ethical conduct, you establish yourself as a person of integrity, and others are naturally drawn to your charm. It's important to note that charm rooted in respect and integrity is not a superficial facade but a genuine reflection of your character. It requires self-reflection, self-awareness, and a commitment to personal growth. Continuously strive to improve yourself, embracing the values that promote respect and integrity. Surround yourself with individuals who exemplify these qualities, as their influence will further reinforce your own commitment.

In summary, charm flourishes when it is built upon a foundation of respect and integrity. Treat others with genuine respect, embracing their diversity and valuing their perspectives. Uphold unwavering integrity by aligning your words and actions and fostering an atmosphere of trust. By embodying respect and integrity in your interactions, you not only enhance your own charm but also create an environment where meaningful connections and lasting relationships can thrive.

Embracing Continuous Growth: A Path to Lasting Charm and Meaningful Relationships

The pursuit of charm and the cultivation of solid relationships are never-ending endeavors. To nurture and enhance your charm, it is essential to embrace the concept of continuous growth. By committing to personal development and self-improvement, you embark on a transformative journey that will enrich your interactions and strengthen your relationships. Engage in regular self-reflection, taking the time to evaluate your interactions, behaviors, and communication styles. Consider the impact of your words and actions on others and seek opportunities for growth. Acknowledge your strengths and celebrate them, while also identifying areas where improvement is needed. By cultivating self-awareness, you gain valuable insights into your own charm and its impact on those around you.

Learn from your experiences, both positive and negative. Celebrate the successes that have resulted from your charm and identify the factors that contributed to those favorable outcomes. Similarly, reflect on instances where your charm may have fallen short or led to unintended consequences. Embrace these opportunities as lessons, allowing them to shape your future interactions and refine your charm. Seek feedback from trusted individuals who can provide honest and constructive insights. Be open to their observations, suggestions, and critiques. Embrace feedback as a valuable tool for growth and use it to fuel your personal development journey. By remaining receptive to feedback, you demonstrate humility and a genuine commitment to improvement.

Adaptability is key in the pursuit of charm. As you grow and evolve, be willing to adjust your approach and communication style to suit different individuals and situations. Recognize that what may have charmed one person may not have the same effect on another. By adapting your interactions to meet the unique needs and preferences of those you engage with, you demonstrate a genuine interest in connecting on a deeper level. Incorporate continuous learning into your life. Seek out new knowledge, perspectives, and experiences that broaden your horizons. Stay informed about current events, engage in meaningful conversations, and explore diverse interests. By expanding your knowledge and understanding, you enrich your interactions and become a more engaging and charismatic individual.

Embrace challenges as opportunities for growth. Stepping outside of your comfort zone allows you to develop new skills, overcome obstacles, and expand your capabilities. Embrace the unknown, take calculated risks, and be resilient in the face of setbacks. Each challenge you overcome strengthens your character and deepens your charm.

Remember, the journey of continuous growth is a lifelong endeavor. Embrace it with enthusiasm and a sense of curiosity. Surround yourself with supportive individuals who inspire and encourage your personal development. Celebrate your progress along the way, recognizing that even small steps forward contribute to your overall growth. In summary, continuous growth is the key to nurturing charm and building meaningful relationships. Embrace self-reflection, learn from your experiences, and adapt your approach. Seek feedback, remain open to learning, and embrace challenges as opportunities for growth. By committing to personal development and continuous growth, you enhance your charm and create a foundation for lasting and meaningful connections with others.

By implementing these strategies and embracing the core principles of charm, you have the potential to cultivate solid and meaningful relationships that greatly enhance both your personal and professional life. These skills empower you to connect with others on a deeper level, fostering trust, respect, and mutual understanding. In the next chapter, we will delve into the significance of confidence and its profound impact on various aspects of your life. Confidence plays a pivotal role in achieving success and happiness, as it influences how you perceive yourself, interact with others, and navigate life's challenges. We will explore practical techniques and insights to help you boost your confidence and unlock your full potential. Stay tuned for an enlightening exploration of confidence and its transformative power.

CHAPTER 8

HOW TO BE MORE CONFIDENT: THE KEY TO SUCCESS AND HAPPINESS

Confidence is a powerful trait that can have a transformative effect on every aspect of your life. In this chapter, we delve into the strategies and techniques that can help you cultivate self-assurance and boost your confidence levels. By understanding the foundations of confidence and learning how to overcome self-doubt and manage social anxiety, you can project an air of confidence that will open doors to success and happiness.

Recognizing and Embracing Your Unique Strengths:

The first step in developing self-confidence is to consciously acknowledge and appreciate your individual strengths and talents. Take the time to reflect on your past accomplishments and the skills you have honed throughout your life's journey. Recognize the inherent value that you bring to a variety of situations and consider how your unique strengths can positively contribute to your personal and professional growth. By recognizing your strengths, you gain a deeper understanding of your abilities and potential. This self-awareness allows you to leverage your strengths effectively, maximizing their impact in different areas of your life. Embracing your strengths means accepting them wholeheartedly, without downplaying or diminishing their signify-cance. It involves celebrating your talents and accepting yourself as a capable individual. Building a solid foundation of self-confidence begins with embracing the positive qualities and attributes that make you who you are. By acknowledging and appreciating your strengths, you cultivate a sense of self-worth and belief in your abilities. This self-assurance radiates through your actions and interactions, influencing how you approach challenges and opportunities.

When you recognize and embrace your strengths, you develop a strong sense of self-identity. You become more grounded in your capabilities and are better equipped to navigate through life's ups and downs. Understanding your strengths empowers you to make informed decisions and pursue paths that align with your natural inclinations and talents. Furthermore, recognizing your strengths allows you to tap into your full potential. It enables you to optimize your performance and achieve greater success in various aspects of your life. By capitalizing on your strengths, you can bring unique perspectives, innovative solutions, and valuable contributions to different situations and environments.

It is important to note that everyone possesses a distinct set of strengths, and there is no one-size-fits-all approach to recognizing and embracing them. Some strengths may be evident and easily recognizable, while others may require deeper exploration and self-reflection. Take the time to identify both your obvious and hidden strengths, as they all play a role in shaping your self-confidence. Embracing your strengths also involves acknowledging that they can evolve and grow over time. As you continue to learn and acquire new experiences, you may discover additional strengths or enhance existing ones. Remain open to growth and embrace opportunities for personal development. By continually nurturing and expanding your strengths, you set yourself up for continuous growth and self-improvement. In summary, recognizing and embracing your unique strengths is a vital component of building self-confidence. By reflecting on your accomplishments, skills, and the value you bring to different situations, you can develop a deep appreciation for your capabilities. Embracing your strengths involves accepting and celebrating them, allowing them to guide your actions and decisions. By acknowledging and leveraging your strengths, you empower yourself to navigate life's challenges with resilience and a strong sense of self-assurance.

Harnessing the Power of Positive Self-Talk:

Your internal dialogue greatly influences your self-confidence and overall mindset. Take a moment to observe the thoughts and beliefs that flow through your mind on a daily basis. Are they predominantly negative or uplifting? To cultivate self-confidence, it is crucial to replace negative self-talk with positive and empowering statements. Instead of dwelling on your perceived weaknesses, consciously shift your focus to your abilities and past successes. Remind yourself of the challenges you have overcome and the achievements you have accomplished. By reframing your thoughts and highlighting your strengths, you can transform your self-perception and boost your confidence.

Affirmations play a powerful role in rewiring your mindset and reinforcing positive self-talk. These are short, affirmative statements that reflect your desired qualities or outcomes. Create a list of affirmations that resonate with you and align with your goals. Repeat them to yourself regularly, especially during moments of self-doubt or when facing challenges. Affirmations can help counteract negative thoughts, build self-belief, and cultivate a can-do attitude. Incorporating positive self-talk into your daily routine is an ongoing practice that requires mindfulness and persistence. Whenever you catch yourself engaging in negative self-talk, pause and consciously reframe the thought into a positive affirmation. For example, if you find yourself thinking, "I'm not good enough for this opportunity," replace it with, "I am capable and deserving of this opportunity, and I will give it my best."

It's important to note that positive self-talk is not about denying or ignoring challenges and areas for improvement. Rather, it is about adopting a constructive and encouraging mindset that allows you to approach obstacles with resilience and confidence. Recognize that setbacks and failures are part of the learning process and view them as opportunities for growth rather than personal shortcomings. Consistency is key when it comes to cultivating positive self-talk. Make it a habit to practice self-awareness and monitor your thoughts regularly. Surround yourself with supportive influences, whether it's through inspirational books, podcasts, or positive-minded individuals. Engage in activities that boost your self-esteem and reinforce your belief in your capabilities.

As you integrate positive self-talk into your life, you will notice a shift in your mindset and self-confidence. You will become more resilient in the face of challenges and setbacks, as your inner dialogue encourages you to persist and learn from experiences. Positive self-talk not only enhances your self-confidence but also positively impacts your overall well-being and outlook on life. In summary, the power of positive self-talk cannot be underestimated in building self-confidence. By replacing negative thoughts with affirmations and focusing on your abilities and past successes, you can rewire your mindset and cultivate a can-do attitude. Consistency and self-awareness are key to maintaining a positive internal dialogue. Embrace the transformative impact of positive self-talk and watch as your confidence soars, empowering you to overcome obstacles and embrace new opportunities.

Harnessing the Power of Achievable Goals:

Setting clear and attainable goals is a vital component of building confidence. When you have a vision of what you want to achieve, breaking it down into smaller, manageable steps is key. By doing so, you can create a roadmap that guides your actions and provides a sense of direction. Start by clearly defining your long-term goal. What is it that you want to accomplish? Be specific and make sure your goal is measurable so that you can track your progress. For example, if your long-term goal is to start your own business, you might break it down into smaller goals such as conducting market research, developing a business plan, and securing funding.

Once you have your long-term goal in mind, focus on setting achievable short-term goals. These goals should be realistic and within your reach. By breaking down your journey into smaller steps, you not only make it more manageable but also increase your chances of success. Achieving these smaller goals will provide a sense of accomplishment and boost your confidence. Celebrate your milestones along the way. When you reach a significant milestone or complete a step towards your goal, take the time to acknowledge and reward yourself. Celebrating these achievements reinforces a positive mindset and reinforces your belief in your capabilities. It serves as a reminder that you are making progress and moving closer to your ultimate goal.

It's important to remember that setbacks and obstacles are a natural part of any journey. If you encounter challenges along the way, reassess your approach and adjust your goals if necessary. Be flexible and willing to adapt as you learn and grow. Embrace failure as an opportunity for learning and refinement, rather than a reflection of your worth or abilities. By approaching setbacks with resilience and a growth mindset, you can maintain your confidence and continue moving forward. Regularly review and reassess your goals to ensure they remain relevant and aligned with your aspirations. As you achieve your goals and gain confidence, consider setting new, more ambitious ones. By continuously challenging yourself, you can push beyond your comfort zone and expand your capabilities.

Lastly, seek support and accountability. Share your goals with trusted friends, family members, or mentors who can provide encouragement and hold you accountable. Their support can help you stay motivated and focused, especially during challenging times. In summary, setting achievable goals is a powerful strategy for building confidence. Break down your long-term goals into smaller, manageable steps and celebrate your milestones along the way. Embrace setbacks as learning opportunities and be willing to adjust your goals if needed. Regularly review and reassess your goals to ensure they remain relevant and challenging. With each achievement, your confidence will grow, empowering you to tackle more significant challenges and achieve success.

Embracing the Power of Growth: Stepping Outside Your Comfort Zone

Confidence is not built by staying within the boundaries of your comfort zone; it flourishes when you challenge yourself and explore new horizons. By consciously seeking opportunities to expand your comfort zone, you can unlock your true potential and cultivate unwavering self-assurance. One way to expand your comfort zone is to embrace the unknown and try new things. Identify areas of interest or skills you've always wanted to develop and take the leap. Whether it's learning a new language, participating in public speaking engagements, or taking on a leadership role, each endeavor will stretch your abilities and broaden your experiences.

Taking calculated risks is another key aspect of stepping outside your comfort zone. Assess the potential rewards and consequences of a decision or action and make an informed choice to move forward. By challenging the status quo and venturing into uncharted territories, you open doors to new opportunities and experiences that can fuel your confidence. Embrace opportunities for personal and professional growth that push your boundaries. Seek out challenges that may initially seem daunting but offer the potential for substantial growth. Engage in activities that require you to learn new skills or face your fears. Each time you conquer a challenge or overcome a fear, your confidence will soar, and you'll realize the vast reservoir of strength and resilience within you.

It's important to note that stepping outside your comfort zone doesn't mean diving headfirst into the unknown without preparation. Take a thoughtful and deliberate approach by setting realistic goals and breaking them down into manageable steps. This will help you navigate the process and maintain a sense of control and focus. Be open to learning from your experiences, regardless of the outcome. Success will boost your confidence, while failures provide valuable lessons and opportunities for growth. Embrace the mindset of continuous improvement and view setbacks as steppingstones on your path to success. Each experience, whether positive or negative, contributes to your personal and professional development, shaping you into a more resilient and confident individual.

Remember to celebrate your achievements and milestones along the way. Recognize the progress you've made and acknowledge the courage it took to step outside your comfort zone. Reward yourself for your efforts, no matter how small, as this reinforces positive behavior and motivates you to keep pushing forward. Surround yourself with a supportive network of friends, mentors, or like-minded individuals who encourage and inspire you to step outside your comfort zone. Seek their guidance and perspective, as they can provide valuable insights and help you navigate challenges. By intentionally expanding your comfort zone, you break free from self-imposed limitations and open yourself up to a world of endless possibilities. With each step taken outside your comfort zone, you build resilience, adaptability, and confidence. Embrace the discomfort, embrace the growth, and watch your confidence soar to new heights.

Nurturing Your Inner Strength: The Importance of Self-Care for Building Confidence

In the pursuit of confidence, it's essential not to overlook the crucial role that self-care plays in shaping our overall well-being. Taking intentional steps to prioritize and care for your physical and mental health can provide a solid foundation for building lasting confidence. One vital aspect of self-care is ensuring that you get enough restorative sleep. A good night's sleep allows your mind and body to recharge, improving your mood, cognitive function, and overall well-being. Make it a priority to establish a consistent sleep routine and create a peaceful sleep environment that promotes relaxation and quality rest.

Nourishing your body with nutritious meals is another integral part of self-care. A well-balanced diet provides the fuel your body needs to function optimally. Fueling yourself with wholesome foods not only supports your physical health but also has a positive impact on your mental well-being. Aim to include a variety of fruits, vegetables, lean proteins, and whole grains in your meals to ensure you're giving your body the nutrients it requires. Regular physical exercise is not only beneficial for your physical health but also for building confidence. Engaging in physical activities you enjoy helps reduce stress, boosts your mood, and enhances your overall self-image. Find activities that resonate with you, whether it's jogging, dancing, swimming, or practicing yoga. Consistency is key, so aim for regular exercise sessions that suit your schedule and fitness level.

In addition to taking care of your physical health, nurturing your mental well-being is equally important. Incorporating mindfulness or meditation practices into your daily routine can help calm your mind, reduce stress, and enhance self-awareness. Taking moments of stillness to focus on your breath or engage in mindful activities can provide a sense of grounding and inner peace, fostering a positive mindset and boosting your self-confidence. Self-care also involves setting healthy boundaries and prioritizing activities that bring you joy and relaxation. Identify hobbies or interests that energize you and make time for them regularly. Engaging in activities that you love and that align with your passions helps you reconnect with yourself and nourish your soul. Remember, self-care is not selfish; it's a necessary investment in your well-being. By taking care of yourself, you are better equipped to handle life's challenges and approach them with confidence. Prioritize self-care as an essential part of your daily routine, creating a nurturing environment that supports your physical, mental, and emotional health.

Lastly, seek support when needed. Surround yourself with a network of trusted individuals who uplift and encourage you. Reach out to friends, family, or professionals when you require guidance or assistance. Building a support system allows you to share your experiences, seek advice, and receive the encouragement and validation that can strengthen your confidence. Incorporating self-care practices into your life is an ongoing journey of self-discovery and self-love. By prioritizing your well-being, you cultivate the inner strength necessary to face challenges, embrace your true potential, and build unshakable confidence from within. Take the time to care for yourself and watch as your confidence blooms and flourishes.

Navigating Social Anxiety: Building Confidence One Step at a Time

Social anxiety can be a significant barrier to building confidence, particularly in social settings. However, it's important to recognize that many people experience varying degrees of anxiety in social situations. By adopting strategies to manage and overcome social anxiety, you can gradually build confidence and feel more at ease when interacting with others.

The first step in managing social anxiety is to challenge negative thoughts and replace them with more realistic and positive perspectives. Often, individuals with social anxiety engage in self-critical thinking and assume the worst-case scenarios in social situations. Take a moment to identify and question these negative thoughts. Ask yourself if they are based on evidence or if there are alternative, more positive interpretations. Practice reframing your thoughts by focusing on your strengths, past successes, and the potential for positive outcomes in social interactions. To gradually expose yourself to social situations, it can be helpful to start with smaller gatherings or one-on-one interactions.

Begin by engaging in activities or events where you feel relatively comfortable, such as meeting a close friend for coffee or attending a small group gathering with people you trust. As you become more comfortable in these settings, gradually challenge yourself to participate in slightly larger or more unfamiliar social situations.

Setting achievable goals for each social interaction can also be beneficial. Start with small, specific goals that are within your comfort zone. For example, you might aim to initiate a conversation with one new person at an event or share your opinion during a group discussion. As you achieve these goals, acknowledge, and celebrate your progress, which will help boost your confidence and motivation to continue expanding your comfort zone. It's important to remember that building confidence takes time and patience. Don't be too hard on yourself if you experience setbacks or moments of increased anxiety. Instead, view these instances as opportunities for growth and learning. Reflect on what you can learn from each experience and use it to adjust your approach moving forward.

Additionally, practicing relaxation techniques can help manage anxiety in social situations. Deep breathing exercises, progressive muscle relaxation, or mindfulness techniques can help you stay calm and centered. Engaging in these practices before and during social interactions can help reduce anxiety and promote a sense of calmness and control.

Seeking support from trusted individuals can also be instrumental in managing social anxiety. Consider confiding in a close friend, family member, or mental health professional who can offer guidance, understanding, and encouragement. They can provide a safe space for you to express your feelings, fears, and successes, and offer valuable insights and coping strategies. Remember, building confidence in social situations is a gradual process. Be patient with yourself and celebrate each step forward, no matter how small it may seem. With practice, perseverance, and the implementation of these strategies, you can gradually overcome social anxiety, develop greater confidence, and enjoy more fulfilling social interactions.

Harnessing the Power of Body Language and Presence: Enhancing Confidence and Influence

Your body language speaks volumes about your level of confidence and can significantly impact how others perceive you. By mastering the art of body language and presence, you can enhance your self-assurance and positively influence the way others interact with you. Here are some strategies to help you project confidence through your body language and presence.

Stand tall and maintain an open posture:

Good posture exudes confidence and presence. Stand tall with your shoulders back and your head held high. Avoid slouching or crossing your arms, as this can convey defensiveness or insecurity. Instead, adopt an open and relaxed posture that signals approachability and self-assurance.

Make eye contact:

Establishing and maintaining eye contact is crucial for projecting confidence. When engaging in conversations, maintain eye contact with the person you're speaking to. This demonstrates active listening, attentiveness, and a sense of self-assurance. However, be mindful of cultural differences and ensure your eye contact is respectful and appropriate in different contexts.

Use assertive and confident communication:

Your tone of voice and the way you express yourself verbally also play a significant role in projecting confidence. Speak clearly, with a moderate pace and volume that commands attention. Avoid mumbling or speaking too softly, as this can undermine your message. Practice using assertive language that conveys confidence and authority while still being respectful and considerate of others.

Be mindful of your gestures:

Gestures can complement your verbal communication and add emphasis to your message. Use purposeful and controlled gestures that align with your words. Avoid fidgeting, excessive hand movements, or gestures that may convey nervousness or uncertainty. Instead, strive for natural and confident gestures that reinforce your message and engage your audience.

Develop an aura of calmness and composure:

Confidence is not just about external behaviors; it also stems from inner calmness and composure. Practice relaxation techniques, such as deep breathing or meditation, to help manage any nervousness or anxiety you may feel. Cultivating a sense of inner peace and tranquility will help you project a calm and confident demeanor to those around you.

Be present and engaged:

When interacting with others, strive to be fully present in the moment. Avoid distractions and show genuine interest in the conversation or activity at hand. Active listening, nodding, and providing thoughtful responses demonstrate your attentiveness and engagement. This level of presence and engagement not only boosts your confidence but also enhances the quality of your interactions.

Practice, observe, and adapt:

Building confidence in your body language and presence takes practice. Observe confident individuals you admire and take note of their posture, gestures, and overall presence. Pay attention to how they communicate and connect with others. Incorporate these observations into your own style while still staying true to yourself. Continually seek feedback from trusted individuals who can provide valuable insights and suggestions for improvement.

By consciously working on your body language and presence, you can project confidence and influence others in a positive way. Remember, building confidence in these areas is a gradual process, so be patient and persistent. With time and practice, you will develop a strong and impactful presence that enhances your self-assurance and leaves a lasting impression on those around you.

Building Confidence through Competence: Investing in Knowledge and Skills

Confidence and competence go hand in hand. Building competence in areas that matter to you is an effective way to boost your confidence. By investing time and effort in developing your skills and knowledge, you lay a strong foundation for self-assurance and success. Here are some strategies to help you build competence and enhance your confidence.

Identify your areas of interest:

Start by identifying the areas of knowledge or skills that you are passionate about. What subjects or activities do you enjoy and want to excel in? By focusing on your interests, you can maintain motivation and enthusiasm as you work on developing your competence.

Set clear learning goals:

Once you have identified your areas of interest, set clear and achievable learning goals. Break down your goals into smaller milestones that you can work towards. This will help you stay focused and track your progress as you develop your competence.

Seek out learning opportunities:

Take advantage of various learning opportunities available to you. Enroll in relevant courses or workshops, attend conferences or seminars, and participate in webinars or online communities related to your chosen areas of competence. These opportunities provide valuable knowledge, insights, and connections that can accelerate your learning and growth.

Read and research:

Expand your knowledge by reading books, articles, research papers, and industry publications. Stay updated with the latest trends and developments in your field of interest. Engage in critical thinking and reflect on the information you consume to deepen your understanding and enhance your competence.

Seek mentorship and guidance:

Connect with experienced individuals who can serve as mentors or guides in your areas of interest. Seek their advice, insights, and feedback on your progress. Their guidance and support can provide valuable perspectives, help you avoid common pitfalls, and accelerate your learning journey.

Practice and apply your skills:

Building competence requires practice and practical application. Look for opportunities to apply your skills in real-life situations. Take on projects, volunteer, or find internships that allow you to put your knowledge into action. Embrace challenges and learn from both successes and failures, as they are essential for growth and building confidence.

Embrace a growth mindset:

Adopt a growth mindset, believing that your abilities and intelligence can be developed through effort and persistence. Embrace challenges as opportunities for learning and view setbacks as stepping stones to success. Cultivate a positive attitude towards continuous learning and improvement, which will fuel your confidence and drive for competence.

Celebrate achievements and milestones:

As you make progress in building competence, celebrate your achievements and milestones along the way. Acknowledge your growth, whether it's mastering a new skill, completing a challenging project, or gaining recognition in your field. Celebrating these accomplishments boosts your confidence and reinforces your belief in your abilities.

Remember, building competence is an ongoing journey that requires dedication and perseverance. Be patient with yourself and enjoy the process of continuous learning and growth. As you develop your skills and knowledge, your confidence will naturally grow, empowering you to take on new challenges and achieve your goals with self-assurance.

Surrounding Yourself with Positive Influences: Boosting Confidence through Supportive Relationships

The people we surround ourselves with can have a profound impact on our confidence levels and overall well-being. Building a supportive network of positive influences can greatly enhance your self-assurance and help you overcome self-doubt. Here are some strategies for surrounding yourself with positive influences to boost your confidence:

Identify supportive individuals:

Take stock of the people in your life and identify those who uplift and support you. Look for individuals who genuinely believe in your abilities, encourage your personal growth, and provide constructive feedback. These individuals should have a positive influence on your self-esteem and confidence.

Cultivate positive relationships:

Once you have identified supportive individuals, invest time and effort in cultivating positive relationships with them. Nurture these connections through regular communication, shared experiences, and mutual support. Surrounding yourself with people who uplift and inspire you will create an environment conducive to personal growth and enhanced confidence.

Seek out mentors and role models:

Look for mentors and role models who embody the qualities and achievements you aspire to. These individuals can provide valuable guidance, share their experiences, and inspire you to reach new heights. Engage with them through mentorship programs, professional networks, or industry events. Their wisdom and encouragement will help fuel your confidence.

Join supportive communities:

Seek out communities or groups that align with your interests, goals, or values. These communities can be online or offline and provide a platform for connection, collaboration, and support. Engaging with like-minded individuals who share similar passions and ambitions can foster a sense of belonging and boost your confidence.

Distance yourself from negativity:

Take a critical look at your social circle and assess whether any individuals or relationships consistently bring you down or undermine your self-confidence. It's essential to set healthy boundaries and distance yourself from negative influences. Surrounding yourself with positive and supportive people will create a more uplifting and empowering environment.

Build a diverse support network:

Aim to build a diverse support network that includes individuals from different backgrounds, perspectives, and areas of expertise. This diversity will expose you to varied insights and broaden your horizons, fostering personal growth and expanding your confidence.

Be a positive influence yourself:

Remember that you have the power to be a positive influence on others as well. Offer support, encouragement, and constructive feedback to those around you. By uplifting others, you create a positive ripple effect and contribute to a supportive community that fosters confidence and personal growth.

Practice gratitude:

Express gratitude for the positive influences in your life. Regularly acknowledge and appreciate the supportive individuals who contribute to your confidence and well-being. Cultivating a mindset of gratitude strengthens your relationships and fosters a positive and supportive environment.

Surrounding yourself with positive influences is a powerful strategy for boosting your confidence. By seeking out supportive individuals, cultivating positive relationships, and being mindful of the company you keep, you can create an uplifting and empowering network that fuels your self-assurance and helps you overcome self-doubt. Remember, confidence is contagious, and by surrounding yourself with positive influences, you not only benefit personally but also contribute to the growth and confidence of those around you.

Embracing Failure as a Catalyst for Growth: Building Confidence through Resilience

Failure is a natural and inevitable part of life's journey. It is essential to recognize that failure does not define your worth or diminish your confidence. Instead, viewing failures as valuable learning experiences can transform them into steppingstones for personal and professional growth. Here are some strategies to embrace failure as a catalyst for growth and strengthen your confidence:

Shift your perspective:

Rather than seeing failure as a negative outcome, reframe it as an opportunity for growth and learning. Understand that even the most successful individuals have experienced failures along their paths. Embrace failure as a natural part of the learning process and an essential steppingstone towards success.

Analyze and learn:

When faced with failure, take the time to reflect on what went wrong. Identify the factors that contributed to the outcome and analyze the lessons that can be gleaned from the experience. By understanding the root causes, you can develop strategies to overcome similar challenges in the future.

Embrace resilience:

Cultivate resilience in the face of failure. Recognize that setbacks are temporary and that you can bounce back stronger. Embracing resilience means staying committed to your goals, maintaining a positive mindset, and persevering through adversity. Each time you overcome a failure, your confidence will grow, and your resilience will strengthen.

Extract lessons and adjust:

Use failure as an opportunity to extract valuable lessons. Identify the specific skills, knowledge, or strategies that need improvement. Adapt your approach and make the necessary adjustments based on the insights gained from your failure. This growth mindset will not only enhance your confidence but also increase your chances of future success.

Celebrate progress and small wins:

It's important to acknowledge and celebrate your progress, even in the face of failure. Recognize the smaller victories and milestones along your journey. By focusing on your growth and the positive steps you've taken, you reinforce your self-confidence and build momentum towards future accomplishments.

Surround yourself with support:

Seek support from a network of positive influences, such as friends, mentors, or support groups. Share your experiences and challenges with those who understand and can provide encouragement and guidance. Their perspective and insights can help you maintain confidence during difficult times.

Maintain a growth mindset:

Cultivate a growth mindset that embraces challenges, persistence, and continuous learning. Understand that failure is not a reflection of your abilities, but rather an opportunity to refine and expand them. Embrace the belief that with effort and dedication, you can overcome obstacles and achieve success.

Practice self-compassion:

Be kind to yourself in the face of failure. Avoid self-criticism and negative self-talk. Treat yourself with compassion and understanding, recognizing that everyone experiences setbacks. By practicing self-compassion, you foster a positive relationship with yourself and cultivate a resilient and confident mindset. Embracing failure as a catalyst for growth is a transformative mindset that can significantly impact your confidence. By shifting your perspective, analyzing failures, embracing resilience, and extracting valuable lessons, you'll develop a strong sense of self-assurance. Remember, failure is not the end, but rather a steppingstone on your path to success.

Remember, building confidence is a gradual process that requires patience and self-compassion. It's important to embrace the journey and acknowledge that it may take time to fully develop your confidence. Celebrate every small step forward along the way, as each accomplishment contributes to your overall growth. Consistency and practice are key to building confidence. Keep implementing the strategies and techniques we've discussed, and don't be discouraged by setbacks or moments of self-doubt. Trust in the process and believe in your ability to grow and improve.

Maintain a growth mindset as you continue your confidence-building journey. Embrace challenges as opportunities for growth and learning. Approach each situation with curiosity and a willingness to step outside your comfort zone. Remember that every experience, both successes and failures, contributes to your personal and professional development. Seek out resources and tools that can support your confidence-building efforts. There are numerous books, courses, workshops, and online resources available that provide guidance and techniques for enhancing charisma and confidence. Take advantage of these resources to deepen your understanding, gain new insights, and refine your skills. Surround yourself with a supportive network of friends, mentors, or coaches who believe in your potential and encourage your growth. Share your experiences and challenges with them, as their perspectives and feedback can provide valuable guidance and motivation.

Lastly, be kind to yourself throughout this process. Celebrate your progress and achievements, no matter how small they may seem. Treat yourself with self-compassion and practice positive self-talk. Remind yourself of your worth and the unique qualities that make you special. By consistently practicing these principles and maintaining a growth mindset, you will witness a significant boost in your confidence levels over time. Remember that confidence is not a destination, but an ongoing journey of self-discovery and personal growth. Embrace the tools and resources available to you, and continue to thrive in both your personal and professional endeavors.

CHAPTER 9

TOOLS AND RESOURCES TO HELP YOU BE MORE CHARISMATIC

As you embark on your journey to enhance your charisma, it's essential to have access to the right tools and resources that can support your growth and development. In this chapter, we provide a comprehensive compilation of valuable resources, including books, online courses, podcasts, and practical exercises, to help you become more charis-matic and continue your progress with confidence.

Books on Charisma and Communication:

Books are an excellent resource for gaining in-depth knowledge and practical insights into charisma and effective communication. Here are some highly recommended titles:

- "How to Win Friends and Influence People" by Dale Carnegie: A timeless classic that explores the principles of effective communication and relationship-building.
- "The Charisma Myth: How Anyone Can Master the Art and Science of Personal Magnetism" by Olivia Fox Cabane: An insightful guide that reveals the science behind charisma and provides practical techniques for developing it.
- "Influence: The Psychology of Persuasion" by Robert Cialdini: This book explores the principles of persuasion and influence, offering valuable insights into the art of charismatic communication.

Online Courses and Workshops:

Online courses and workshops provide a structured learning experience that allows you to delve deeper into specific aspects of charisma. Some reputable platforms that offer courses on communication and charisma include:

- Coursera: Offers courses on interpersonal communication, public speaking, and leadership skills.

- Udemy: Provides a wide range of courses on charisma, influence, and effective communication.
- LinkedIn Learning: Offers courses on charismatic leadership, storytelling, and personal branding.

Podcasts and Audio Resources:

Podcasts are a convenient way to expand your knowledge and gain practical tips on the go. Here are a few charisma-focused podcasts to explore:

- "The Art of Charm": Hosted by Jordan Harbinger, this podcast explores various aspects of social dynamics, personal growth, and charisma.
- "The Charisma Coach": In this podcast, Felicia Spahr shares insights and tips on developing charisma and improving communication skills.
- "The Science of Success": While not solely focused on charisma, this podcast delves into the science and psychology of success, offering valuable insights that can enhance your charismatic journey.

Practical Exercises and Activities:

Practice is key to developing and honing your charismatic skills. Here are some exercises and activities you can engage in:

- Role-playing: Practice different social scenarios with a trusted friend or mentor. Experiment with body language, tone of voice, and persuasive techniques.
- Active Listening: Engage in active listening exercises where you focus on truly understanding the other person's perspective, emotions, and needs. Practice asking insightful questions and providing meaningful responses.
- Public Speaking: Join a public speaking club or participate in speaking engagements to build confidence and improve your ability to engage and captivate an audience.
- Networking Events: Attend networking events or social gatherings to practice initiating conversations, building rapport, and leaving a positive impression.

Charisma Building Apps:

In the digital age, there are also apps available to support your charismatic journey. These apps offer interactive exercises, tips, and challenges to help you develop your communication skills and boost your confidence.

- Charisma App: Provides daily exercises and challenges to improve your charisma and communication skills.
- Talk space: An app that connects you with licensed therapists who can assist with social anxiety and self-confidence issues.

Coaching and Mentoring:

Consider seeking the guidance of a professional coach or mentor who specializes in communication and charisma. Working with a skilled mentor can provide personalized guidance, feedback, and support as you navigate your charismatic journey.

Online Communities and Forums:

Engage with like-minded individuals in online communities and forums focused on charisma and personal development. These platforms offer opportunities to share experiences, seek advice, and learn from others who are also on a similar path.

Remember, the tools and resources mentioned here are designed to provide support and enhance your journey, but true growth comes from actively applying what you learn in real-life situations. Embrace the process, remain open to learning, and adapt the techniques that resonate with you the most. The key to developing charisma and confidence lies in consistent practice and application. Take the knowledge and strategies you've gained and put them into action in your daily interactions. Be willing to step out of your comfort zone and apply what you've learned, even if it feels uncomfortable at first.

In addition to the tools and resources mentioned, consider seeking out opportunities for further development. Attend workshops, seminars, or training programs that focus on charisma, communication, and confidence-building. These experiences can provide valuable insights, practical exercises, and feedback to help you refine your skills. Another valuable resource is seeking guidance from mentors or coaches who specialize in charisma and confidence development. They can provide personalized guidance, support, and accountability as you work towards your goals. Their expertise and perspective can offer valuable insights and help you navigate any challenges that arise along the way. Remember to approach your growth with a mindset of curiosity and self-reflection. Continuously evaluate your progress, identify areas for improvement, and celebrate your successes. Embrace a growth mindset that views setbacks as learning opportunities and allows for continuous improvement.

Finally, remember that building charisma and confidence is a lifelong journey. It's important to regularly reassess your goals, refine your skills, and adapt to new situations and challenges. Stay committed to your personal growth and embrace the process as you continue to unlock new levels of success and fulfillment in both your personal and professional life.

CHAPTER 10

FAQS ABOUT CHARISMA

1. Is charisma something you're born with, or can it be developed?

Charisma is a combination of inherent traits and learned skills. While some individuals may naturally possess certain charismatic qualities, charisma can be developed and enhanced through practice and self-awareness. By understanding the principles and techniques of charisma, anyone can cultivate and improve their charismatic abilities.

2. Is charisma only about being outgoing and extroverted?

Charisma is not limited to extroverted personalities. Introverts can also possess charisma by leveraging their unique strengths, such as active listening, thoughtful insights, and authentic connections.

Charisma is about making others feel valued and inspired, regardless of personality type.

3. Can charisma be used to manipulate or deceive others?

Charisma itself is not inherently manipulative or deceptive. However, individuals with charismatic qualities can misuse them for personal gain. It is important to use charisma ethically, with genuine intentions and respect for others. Being aware of the potential for manipulation can help guard against its negative effects.

4. How can I overcome social anxiety and develop charisma?

Overcoming social anxiety and developing charisma go hand in hand. Start by gradually exposing yourself to social situations and practicing active listening and empathy. Seek opportunities to engage in conversations, join social clubs or public speaking groups, and challenge yourself to step out of your comfort zone. Remember, developing charisma is a journey that requires patience and perseverance.

5. What role does body language play in charisma?

Body language is a crucial component of charisma. Nonverbal cues such as maintaining eye contact, having an open posture, and using confident gestures can significantly enhance your charismatic presence. Pay attention to your body language and practice conveying positive and confident signals to others.

6. Can charisma be learned through online courses and books alone?

Online courses and books provide valuable knowledge and techniques, but charisma is ultimately developed through real-life experiences and interactions. Applying what you learn in practical situations, seeking feedback, and continuously refining your skills are essential for true growth in charisma.

7. Does charisma have an age limit?

Charisma knows no age limit. It can be cultivated and developed at any stage of life. Whether you're a teenager, a young professional, or a seasoned individual, you have the capacity to enhance your charisma and make meaningful connections with others.

8. Can charisma positively impact my professional success?

Absolutely! Charisma plays a vital role in professional success. Effective communication, the ability to build rapport, and influence others are highly sought-after skills in the workplace. Charismatic individuals are often more likely to be trusted, respected, and seen as leaders in their fields.

9. Can I be charismatic in different cultural settings?

Cultural contexts may influence the specific expressions of charisma, but the underlying principles remain universal. Developing genuine connections, active listening, and adapting to cultural norms can help you navigate different cultural settings and effectively connect with people from diverse backgrounds.

10. Is it possible to be charismatic while staying true to myself?

Absolutely! Authenticity is a key component of charisma. Being true to yourself and expressing your genuine thoughts and emotions will attract others who appreciate and resonate with your authentic self. Embrace your unique qualities and let your charisma shine through your authentic presence.

By addressing these frequently asked questions, we aim to provide a deeper understanding of charisma and its practical application in your personal and professional life. Remember, developing charisma is a continuous process of self-improvement, self-awareness, and genuine connection with others.

CONCLUSION

SUMMARIZING THE MAIN POINTS AND HIGHLIGHTING THE IMPORTANCE OF CHARISMA IN OUR LIVES

Throughout this book, we have embarked on a journey to explore the fascinating world of charisma and its impact on our lives. We have covered a wide range of topics, delving into the definition of charisma, its psychological and scientific foundations, its benefits, and even its potential pitfalls. We have provided practical tips and advice on how to enhance your own charisma, develop meaningful relationships, and navigate the complexities of social interactions. One of the key takeaways from our exploration is that charisma is not an innate trait reserved for a lucky few, but rather a set of skills and qualities that can be learned, nurtured, and refined over time. Whether you consider yourself an introvert or an extrovert, charisma is within your reach. It's about understanding yourself, connecting with others authentically, and continuously striving for personal growth.

In the introductory chapters, we established the importance of charisma in today's interconnected world. We recognized that effective communication and the ability to connect with others are essential for personal happiness, professional success, and overall well-being. We acknowledge that social anxiety can present challenges, but with the right mindset and tools, it can be overcome. Moving forward, we explored the psychological and scientific aspects of charisma. We discovered the underlying mechanisms that make charisma such a powerful tool, exploring neurological and evolutionary perspectives. Understanding the science behind charisma empowers us to leverage this knowledge and apply it in our daily interactions. We then explored the benefits of being charismatic, uncovering how charisma positively impacts various aspects of our lives. We recognized its influence on mental and physical health, personal relationships, and professional success. By embodying charisma, we open doors to opportunities, inspire others, and create a positive ripple effect in our lives and the lives of those around us.

However, we must also acknowledge the potential dark side of charisma. In Chapter 4, we confronted the uncomfortable truth that charisma can be used for manipulation and control. By understanding the warning signs and ethical considerations, we can protect ourselves and others from its negative effects. It is essential to use charisma responsibly, with integrity, and in the service of fostering genuine connections.

In subsequent chapters, we provided practical guidance on how to cultivate charisma. We explored techniques for becoming more likeable and sociable, mastering persuasion and influence, and building solid relationships. We emphasized the importance of body language, active listening, empathy, and authenticity. Through consistent practice and embracing discomfort, we can unlock our innate charm and make lasting impressions on others. We further explored the significance of confidence in charisma. In Chapter 8, we recognized that confidence is a key ingredient in personal and professional success. We explored strategies to overcome self-doubt, manage social anxiety, and project confidence in various situations. By cultivating confidence, we can unlock our true potential, pursue our goals with conviction, and radiate an aura of self-assuredness.

Chapter 9 provided a valuable compilation of tools and resources to support your journey toward becoming more charismatic. From recommended readings and online courses to practical exercises and online communities, these resources offer ongoing support and inspiration. Remember, true growth in charisma comes from consistent practice and real-life application of the principles and techniques discussed. In the final chapter, we addressed frequently asked questions, clarifying common misconceptions and offering practical advice. We emphasized that charisma is not limited by age, personality type, or cultural context. It is a skill set that can be developed by anyone willing to invest time, effort, and self-reflection. As we conclude this book, we want to emphasize the profound impact charisma can have on our lives. By developing our charisma, we can create deeper connections, inspire others, and leave a positive imprint on the world. It is not just about surface-level charm or popularity but rather about fostering genuine connections based on empathy, authenticity, and respect.

Charisma is not a destination but a lifelong journey of self-discovery and growth. As you continue your charismatic journey, remember to be patient and kind to yourself. Celebrate your progress, learn from your setbacks, and remain committed to personal growth.

Charisma is not about perfection but about continuous improvement. So, embrace the principles and techniques shared in this book. Apply them in your daily life, experiment with different approaches, and find what works best for you. Cultivate your charisma with intention, integrity, and a genuine desire to make a positive impact on those around you.

Remember, charisma is not just a tool for personal advancement; it is a way of being that brings joy, fulfillment, and meaningful connections. By embracing your own charisma, you can create a ripple effect of positivity and inspiration in your interactions with others. The world needs more individuals who can authentically connect, inspire, and make a difference. As you embark on your journey to enhance your charisma, remember that you are not alone. The knowledge, insights, and resources shared in this book are here to support you. Embrace your unique qualities, cultivate your charisma, and let your light shine brightly in the world.

www.ingramcontent.com/pod-product-compliance
Lightning Source LLC
Chambersburg PA
CBHW060803050426
42449CB00008B/1508